How I Invented the Internet

A Memoir

How I Invented the Internet

A Memoir

Marilyn Carr

IGUANA

Copyright © 2022 Marilyn Carr
Published by Iguana Books
720 Bathurst Street, Suite 410
Toronto, ON M5S 2R4

All rights reserved. No part of this publication may be reproduced, stored in a retrieval system or transmitted, in any form or by any means, electronic, mechanical, recording or otherwise (except brief passages for purposes of review) without the prior permission of the author.

Publisher: Meghan Behse
Front cover design: Jonathan Relph

ISBN 978-1-77180-568-1 (paperback)
ISBN 978-1-77180-569-8 (epub)

This is an original print edition of *How I Invented the Internet: A Memoir*.

Also by Marilyn Carr

Nowhere like This Place: Tales from a Nuclear Childhood

Praise for *Nowhere like This Place*

"What do you get when you transplant a young girl from Quebec into what could arguably be called the most unique community in all of Canada in the 1960s and watch her grow up there? You get the makings of a very funny and perspective book."
—*North Renfrew Times*

"A coming-of-age book like no other. How could life be normal in a town that wasn't? Carr manages to make you feel like you are there with her, wending her way through a 'manufactured' town, where much like *Alice In Wonderland*, nothing is quite as it seems. Carr's comfort with words is obvious as she helps us laugh along with her descriptions of a childhood and adolescence that we can all relate to. A funny and thoroughly enjoyable read."
—Goodreads.com

"The judges were impressed with the grace and quality of your writing, and remarked as well on your ability to convey humour on the page, comparing it favourably to Terry Fallis."
—Penguin Random House Canada MFA Prize 2020 Finalist

"Marilyn Carr's writing style is fluid and laced with a wry sense of humour that was a delight to read. You came away with a sense of knowing the author as if you had been friends for years. It's an outstanding book and a must read for anyone seeking a journey back in time to their time of youth."
—Chaptersindigo.com

For every woman who has wrecked her pantyhose on computer workstations designed by men.

1

Do Not Fold, Spindle, or Mutilate

<u>1979</u>

Dataline's Toronto office is in a low-rise industrial loft-like space, long before industrial loft-like workplaces are a thing. The windows are sixteen-pane safety-glass panels held together by black wrought-iron mullions. My interview is with Don Kennedy, vice president of operations. I walk up six stairs from the parking lot to the front door. I'm wearing my best interview clothes: a grey skirt suit I got on sale, a blue-striped dress shirt I bought from the boys' department, nylons, and grey pumps. I stumbled on the children's department shirt-shopping thing by accident, after too many attempts to buy something that wasn't a frilly blouse. My pitch-brown hair is cut in a Dorothy Hamill wedge that I'm trying to grow out. Dorothy is so 1976 and here we are six months away from 1980. I carry a brand-new leather briefcase. Completely empty. Not even a sandwich inside.

Fenella, Don's secretary, comes to collect me. She's exactly my height and weight and probably struggles just as much as I do to keep above one hundred pounds. Her blond hair is in a bun secured by a scrunchy, and her silk blouse and wide trousers are both black. She has a clipped English accent and an aloof manner. Don must be very important. Fenella presses the elevator button and we wait in uncomfortable silence for five minutes until the elevator arrives. I guess she doesn't want to reveal company secrets to someone who doesn't yet work here. The door opens excruciatingly slowly and we squish into a space that could fit four people with maximum discomfort. Fenella presses the up button and the elevator lurches, stalls, then proceeds on its ascent.

"That's a relief," she says. "I was stuck in here for most of the day yesterday." The elevator eventually makes it up to the second floor.

The door opens on a room that's dotted with workspaces I assume are for the worker bees, hived off by curved four-foot-tall cloth dividers covered in what looks like indoor-outdoor carpet, but the orange kind not the green kind. The dividers are perched on squat metal feet that are angled directly toward the door. Maybe the dividers are smarter than anyone in this room. The executive offices hug the exterior cinder-block walls, each with a full view of the parking lot. This is not as fancy as it sounds.

The cavernous space is lit by warehouse lights suspended from the fifteen-foot ceiling. Their ribbed industrial glass domes create elongated circles on the floor, as welcoming as searchlights. Fenella and I walk across the room, while men's heads pop up above the cubicle walls like groundhogs checking to see if spring has arrived. Apparently, girls in suits are as rare in these parts as swaths of sunshine in February. Fenella ushers me into Don's office and smiles enigmatically.

Don's short-sleeve dress shirt is accented with a wide tie decorated with orange and pink Hawaiian flowers. His credenza holds a tray overrun with bottles of booze, a random selection of crystal glassware, and a silver ice bucket. His desk has one of those green felt blotters trimmed with leather, which I kind of thought had gone out with the fountain pen, but it's partially obscured by a computer terminal, so maybe it's meant to be ironic. Don's round black ashtray, as big as a hubcap, takes up the rest of the desk. At this moment, there's room for maybe one more butt if someone's completely desperate to stamp out a smoke.

"Have a seat," Don says. I unclench my grip from the handles of my briefcase, set it on the floor in front of Don's desk, and arrange myself with a confident ballet posture aligned with the straight back of the minimalist wooden guest chair. My narrow wool skirt has slits on either side. This seemed like a good idea because they make it easier to walk. I have never sat in this suit. I feel the cold wood on my legs and look down to see that, when sitting in a way I consider to be proper, the slits create a thigh aperture almost all the way to my waist. I slide forward to the edge of the chair and rearrange my legs by crossing them at the ankles. Don is too immersed in his monologue to notice. At least I dearly hope so.

"Let me tell you about the company," Don says. "Dataline was formed three years ago when Joe, our founder, saw an opportunity to provide economical computing power to companies that can't afford their own computer. It's a new business model called timesharing. The way it works is that we have a bunch of types of business software, for accounting and expense reporting and stuff. We rent out the software, the computing power required to run it, and a place to store the data. We also install the terminals so the customers can access the computers, and train them how to use the software we provide. I think the best way to picture it is this: we own the razors and the razorblades. And everyone needs to shave!" He seems very pleased with his analogy. "Your resume says you know Fortran, right?"

"Yes," I say. "I haven't used it in a while, though." Actually, I barely used it in the first place.

* * *

<u>1976</u>

The math building at the University of Waterloo is not normally where I would choose to hang out. Except I am hanging out there. I grew up in Deep River, Ontario, the company town for Atomic Energy of Canada's Chalk River Nuclear Laboratories. A town that only exists because of science. After an unfortunate incident with hydrochloric acid in chemistry class and several near-death experiences with Bunsen burners, the high school guidance counsellor advised it was best for all of us that I stick with English and other subjects that do not involve combustibles or deadly poisons. But everyone else was headed to Waterloo, a university that was invented to churn out engineers, computer scientists, and mathematicians, so I followed like a lemming. And we all know how well that works out. I am mostly here because it has about a ten-thousand-to-one boy-girl ratio. That's not working out so well either. So far, I don't like any of my allotted ten thousand.

Everyone has to take electives outside of their core faculty. These are called "bird" courses because you are supposed to be able to fly through them with your eyes closed. Assuming that birds can fly with their eyes closed. The objective of a bird course is that it not mess with your grade point average. For engineers, the favoured options are Astronomy 101 (dubbed astrology), Psychology 101 (also known as "I'm okay. I don't care about you"), and Philosophy 101 (smirkingly called "I don't think but I still am"). For arts students, the pool of possible electives amounts to Quantum Physics 1A, Introduction to Gene Splicing, Interstellar Mechanics for Rocket Scientists, and Computer Science 101.

I selected Computer Science 101, a vulture of a bird course that requires going brain-to-brain with a flock of IBM 370s. Each IBM computer is as large as a rhinoceros that's sitting on his rear end. A ton and a half, five feet wide, and six feet tall. The rhinoceri sit in a two-thousand-square-foot, purpose-built, climate-controlled room, on raised floors above metal runways where miles of thick coaxial cable hide like rattlesnakes under rocks, ready to short-circuit in a burst of poison sparks. The math-building computer room is in a basement enclave, but you can observe the whirring tapes and flashing lights from two storeys above, courtesy of the plexiglass walls of the hall forming a walkway around the opening that rings the floors below. The computer room is called the red room because the walls and floors are, inexplicably, as bright red as a candy apple. Perhaps as a foil for the stodgy IBM blue of the computers and their accessories, perhaps as a warning to all who enter its sanctum. A bunch of computer operators scurry around, tending to the needs of the beasts. They wear sneakers in deference to the delicate raised flooring, and cardigans in deference to the cooling system set at sixty degrees, Fahrenheit as they mount and dismount tapes the size of reels of movie film.

My CS101 homework drill consists of finding a machine in the keypunch room that doesn't have an Out of Order sign on it, grabbing a bunch of blank cards, including a pink job card and a handful of blue separator cards, and typing out the lines of Fortran I hope will produce the result specified by my assignment. This week, we have to write a program that will sort the alphabet backward. No matter that nobody anywhere has ever said, "I want all the books on the shelf organized from Z to A." But this is a perfectly logical request in the kingdom of IBM.

The keypunch machine has a keyboard laid out just like a typewriter but with a few extra bits around the edges. Luckily, I took typing in high school instead of calculus. The guys at the machines on either side of me scowl at the keys and peck at them with random stabs of random fingers. We sit on black vinyl swivel chairs patched with several generations of electrical tape, which has a tendency to detach and stick to the bum of your jeans.

The line shuffles slowly toward the card reader that sits at the far end of the input/output room. "Did you hear for next week's assignment we have to draw a square and a circle? What kind of sadistic person makes you draw with a computer? I'm in engineering, not something stupid, like arts!" says the guy in front of me. Someone a few steps behind me drops his deck and the cards skitter across the floor. The rest of us freeze in horror, as if his bad luck could rub off. And indeed it could. I double-check the integrity of the elastic holding my deck together.

There, but for the grace of a thin band of rubber, go I. The rest of us help round up his punched cards, thin pieces of cardboard precisely 7⅜ by 3¼ inches, with a bit of the top-left corner missing. Herman Hollerith's invention is still alive and well almost a hundred years after he first designed it, enjoying a healthy second career as the bane of existence for computer science students in 1976. When cards get dropped or otherwise messed up, you have to put them back in the right order by reading the line of type at the top and restoring them to their correct sequence of the lines of code for the program. This is pretty much as fast and easy as putting together a ten-thousand-piece jigsaw puzzle that's all one colour.

It's my turn. The I/O operator takes my program deck and adds it to the top of a stack that rests at a thirty-degree angle against a metal hopper. He pushes a button to load the cards into the reader, and they make a *thwacking* sound as they disappear into the business end. I walk forward to retrieve my deck from the other side of the machine, where they get spit out in piles delineated by their separator cards, then I continue to the end of the room to join the congregation at the output printer, where a huddle of guys is waiting.

All ten of us are dressed identically in Carhartt overalls and striped rugby shirts. My shirt has three types of blue: pastel, sky, and navy. The guy in front of me has green and white. The guy in front of him has yellow and black. The embroidery on the upper left of my shirt says *South 3 Village 1* because it's the official shirt of my residence building. My men's size small comes down to my knees and has to be stuffed into my overalls, reminiscent of how I used to cram my skirt into my snow pants when I was in elementary school. My cuffs are folded back four times at the wrist, and the white collar splays out to my shoulders.

The printout paper is seventeen inches wide and eleven inches tall, with alternating light green and white stripes to differentiate the rows of print, and a tear-away strip on each side, so if you want to be fancy, you can get rid of the holes that attach the paper to the sprockets on the printer. A pile of blank paper sits in a box on the floor behind it, which comes out in an accordion fold, winding its way through the print drum before it exits at the front, recreating its back-and-forth folds as it lands on the output table. The salmon-pink job card at the front of each deck generates the page that separates the jobs so you know which one is yours. I see mine come out of the printer, its nine-inch-tall CARR made up of tiny Cs, As, and Rs. I've nailed this assignment, for sure. I'll be back in my dorm room by seven, with lots of time to read a chapter of *Bleak House* before English class tomorrow morning.

The next two pages chug out. So far, so good. That should be it, then I'm done. Except the two more pages turn into two more pages and two more pages and two more pages and two more pages and two more pages.

"Endless loop!" says the guy in line behind me, with perhaps more enthusiasm than strictly necessary.

"Endless loop!" says the guy behind him and the guy behind him and the guy behind him. This gets the attention of the operator, who looks up from the card loader, hurries over to the printer, uses a key attached to a massive chain hanging from his belt to open a plastic door, and presses a big red button that freezes the output from propagating further. The operator runs back to the card reader, yelling at us with cyber urgency, "I need to know the job number. Now!"

I look over my shoulder toward the door. Is it possible to just slink out? Do I really need to pass Computer Science 101? The math students are snickering.

"I think it must be the girl's," one of them says. Looks like I didn't exactly nail it. So much for an early evening.

I climb the stairs to the third floor of my residence building just after the clock strikes twelve. The fluorescent light above the doorway of my room is lined with blue separator cards that have been crammed underneath its translucent pebbled-plastic diffuser. Hollerith cards are exactly the same width as the florescent strip. The hallway is a mood-lit tunnel, alternating blue and pink, punctuated by a stationary disco-ball effect in places where random holes were punched in the cards. A particularly edgy innovation.

I open the door to my room, fling my book bag on top of my desk, and flop on the bed on top of the scratchy wool blanket my mother bought me last year. She got a deal from the clearance sale at the blanket factory in Petawawa, the one that supplies bedding for the minimum-security correctional facility at Landry Crossing, near the Petawawa Research Forest, just up the highway from the army base. "This will last for years!" she said. Wonderful. It's a shade of yellow almost exactly the same hue as cheap hotdog mustard.

I open *Bleak House* at my bookmark, a scrap of computer-paper holes. There are sixty-seven chapters. There are two hundred pages per chapter, or at least it seems like there are two hundred pages per chapter. My professor said Dickens was paid by the word. He seemed to think that was a good thing. I mean my professor, not Dickens, although I'm guessing Dickens thought it was a good idea too. I only have forty-seven chapters to go before the midterm test. The midterm is in two weeks. Across the room, the Mona Lisa smirks at me. She's on a piece of computer paper taped at the corners to the cinder-block wall. Her near-smile and all the rest of her is fashioned from a mosaic of alphanumeric characters, printed and overprinted via Fortran print statements. Up close, she's a bunch of lowercase letters and symbols. Stand back and she's a work of art.

* * *

1979

Turns out, there weren't many job openings for the 1977 vintage of newly minted philosophers. To be honest, none. I had to decide what to do to become employable, which apparently required a post-graduate degree. I could not decide between law or library science, so I let the universe decide for me. I accepted the first offer that came my way. That's why I obtained a master's degree in library science. The invitation to law school arrived two weeks later. My two years of library studies turned out to be as scintillating as they sound. And despite my class being 99.9% women, most of the professors were men.

The joke going around was "Why are male librarians like dead fish? Because they all rise to the top." I learned a lot though. I learned how to research stuff, and that's bound to come in handy. I learned that nobody really knows what librarians do (except, everyone knows what the male librarians do, which is preside over important libraries). If you are a run-of-the-mill female librarian people wonder (sometimes with their inside voice) why you need a master's degree to shelve books. But now it was time for me to get a real job. Time to start librarian-ing. Or is it librarian-ating? Librarian-izing? The University of Toronto campus recruiting office and job board are in the basement of Robarts Library, also known as Fort Book, in honour of its brutalist pyramid-shaped concrete façade and corresponding maximum-security-prison interior décor. I descend the cinder-block stairs to a slate-grey door that protects the sanctity of the economic opportunities. It has a small frosted window on top, lest jobless students prematurely behold the wonders within. I push the door. Then pull the door. Then push again and pull again, until I notice a button on the wall to the left of the door. Press to Open, it says. I'm starting to feel like Alice in Wonderland, expecting to drop into an abyss once the door opens.

The recruiting office has bulletin boards on every wall, papered with job postings. It reeks of Gestetner machine fluid, like a room full of leaking felt pens. I make my way around the room counterclockwise, trying to locate the library jobs. The wall starts with architecture and continues through to biohazards. Aha, alphabetic. I mentally run through the letters from A to K, taking care to allow for large swaths of real estate for dentists, doctors, and engineers. My destination should be somewhere three-quarters along the back wall. Unless they're using M for medicine instead of D for doctor. And what if immunologists are posted under I instead of D or M? This would probably be a lot easier if I wasn't a librarian.

I find the L section. Labour lawyer, landscape architect, laser engineer. Okay. Clearly, even though the recruiting office is located in the library, nobody here has ever heard of subject classification. I continue scanning the boards, and there it is! Librarians. Right after the liaison engineer section. Whatever they are. I immediately feel superior to labour lawyers, landscape architects, and laser engineers. Good luck finding a job posting!

Here we go. Children's librarian. That's where you hold court in front of preschoolers, reading *Green Eggs and Ham* until you never want to eat eggs again. Definitely not. Reference librarian. That's where you tell people where to find the bathroom. And where you patrol the room full of books that no one's allowed to take from the room, being vigilant of people ripping pages out of encyclopedias or trying to hide their bologna sandwiches under the edge of the reading table, because if they leave for lunch, they'll lose their spot. Um, not so much. Cataloguer. That's where you figure out where the books should live, so people can find them on the shelf, then take them off the shelf, so that library workers can put them back on the shelf. And so on and so on and so on. Big snore. But wait, what's this? Systems librarian. *Computer timesharing company seeks librarian to manage our software portfolio. Must know Fortran.* The address is just up the street from my graduate residence. I use the public Gestetner machine in the middle of the room to make a copy of the posting, then replace it on the bulletin board. Under *S* for systems. Right above the systems engineer ad, slightly obscured by a request for a systems analyst. That should do it. If anyone from my class is going to get this job, it's going to be me.

* * *

Don tells me there are six DEC 10 midframe computers housed on the top floor of the Dataline building. "Do you know anything about DEC computers?" he asks. I tell him that we only used IBMs at Waterloo. "Well, no worries," he says. "We can de-program you." He snickers and gives me a big wink. I do not get the joke. "As you know, DEC is the second-largest computer manufacturer after IBM. As you also know, all computer companies must have three letters." Don snickers again. I don't get this joke, either. "The DEC 10 is also known as the PDP 10. It's a midframe, which is a mainframe, only smaller. That's why we can fit six of them upstairs. The DEC 10 was also built specifically for timesharing. When there's a critical mass of users, the DEC computers smooth out the bursts of processing requests and slice the time waiting for disks and tapes. That's why it's called timesharing. But we only make money if all six of our machines are whirring like tops. Each of them cost a million dollars, and building out the computer room cost another million. Let me take you on a tour."

Don leads the way out of his office. I pick up my briefcase and hurry after him. We walk to the middle of the floor, where there are two enclosed spaces. He points to the first one and says, "This is the library where we keep all the computer manuals and programming books. Organizing them and keeping track of where they are is one half of your job." He tells me the second room is the terminal room used to communicate with the computer operators. "That's the second part of your job: moving stuff around on the computers." Sure thing. Messing with millions of dollars' worth of hardware every day. "I can't show you the third floor, though. Nobody is allowed up there except the operators," says Don. Nice. Messing with millions of dollars of invisible hardware every day.

We continue our circumnavigation of the second floor, walking past the sales corner, the human resources niche, and the technical writing department. As we go by, all eyes follow me like I'm a deer trying to cross the road and they're the headlights bearing down on me. We stroll the gauntlet back to Don's office as he chitchats with the staff. "How about those Blue Jays? Hey, John, are you parked in the wrong spot again? Ted, I need your expense report by Friday." Not once does Don introduce me or refer to my existence.

Finally, he circles back to his office, sits down at his desk, and motions me back to my chair. "Can you start in a week? Do you have any questions for me? Is thirteen thousand okay?"

Other than the one about Fortran, Don has not asked me a single question about my qualifications and experience, and I have barely uttered a word except "Nice to meet you." But. Thirteen thousand dollars. More than a thousand a month. My own library. "Sure," I say. "I'll see you in a week." I shake his hand, heft my empty briefcase, and wait for Fenella to escort me out. We get back in the elevator, which makes the reverse trip even more slowly than the ascent. Fenella and I stand shoulder-to-shoulder in silence for most of the ride.

Just as the door opens, she says, "Wow. I can't believe Don finally found somebody for the librarian job. He's had that ad up for at least four months already."

2

Operating Assumptions

<u>1979</u>

The house at 120 Bedford Road has been carved into apartments but still retains vestiges of its former regal charm. Mr. Behrens, the landlord, looks like he's at least fifty. He has a weird beard that doesn't have the moustache part, and he wears old-guy clothes: wide-wale corduroys and a cardigan with leather patches on the elbows. Mr. Behrens says he inherited the property from his mother. I hope she isn't in a freezer in the basement. He shows me around, speaking in a murmur so as not to disturb the other tenants nor the ghosts of tenants past, murdered or not. He leads me up the grand staircase that hugs the wall shared with the house next door, with treads shod in the hush of plush emerald-green carpet. We rise for two landings. My new apartment is on the second floor, at the front of the house. I can move in next week.

My apartment is a studio. A studio is a fancy name for a rental with no bedroom. My living room is my bedroom. My bedroom is my living room. My couch must also be my bed. I don't care. At least I'll have a living room and a bedroom and my own kitchen and my own bathroom. And I actually have my own fireplace, which looks like an upside-down funnel and sits about a foot out from the main wall. It's burnt orange. I hope that *burnt* remains just a paint colour.

The first thing I'll need is a bed. And a sofa. Or actually, a sofa bed. I'm guessing The Bay will have something suitable. I dodge the ice-cream-licking meanderers and double-parked baby strollers as I walk over to Yonge and Bloor. The late-spring weather has brought out the city's worst clothing choices: flimsy Adidas running shorts, tube tops, plastic sandals. And that's just the guys. I take the elevator to the furniture section on the top floor of the department store. It opens on a showroom full of living room, bedroom, and dining room dioramas. Would I find the sofa beds in the living room section or the bedroom section? I cannot easily answer this question, but the hovering salesman can. "Over in the far left, miss," he says. He follows me as I make my way to a dim corner. He points to a brown velour two-seater and tells me it's the best seller.

"I don't want brown," I say. "I want beige. Beige is my colour scheme."

"Just a suggestion," he says. "This will be your main piece of furniture. You'll sit on it, sleep on it, eat pizza on it, and probably drink red wine on it."

No way I'm getting brown. I choose a sleek modern couch with upholstery that looks like linen, textured and subtly nuanced, with alternating stripes of light and dark beige. Mary Tyler Moore would approve. The salesman writes up the order. "Scotchgard?" he asks.

I nod. Mary would definitely get Scotchgard.

* * *

Moving day in June is sweaty and sweltering, and for good measure, thunder is rumbling in the west. I sit on the floor of my empty apartment with my back against the living room wall, thumbing through the latest *Cosmopolitan* magazine, waiting for the delivery van. *Any time between nine and four*, they said. The phone installer guy might show up too. *Any time between nine and four*, they said. In the meantime, I set up my stereo. My brother sold me his old Fisher with a turntable, woofer, subwoofer, receiver, and everything. He was too cheap to give it to me. *I paid two hundred bucks for it*, he said. Right. Four years ago. I have three albums: *Fleetwood Mac* by Fleetwood Mac, *My Aim Is True* by Elvis Costello, and *Tupelo Honey* by Van Morrison. I will have everything I need once the couch and phone get here.

 I don't have a watch. I've never worn a watch. Not wearing a watch makes me carefree and artsy. Not wearing a watch means I have no idea what time it is. The clock on the kitchen stove says noon. Or maybe midnight. It hasn't budged since I got here. But once Elvis has sung "Alison" about five times, my doorbell rings. I let the doorbell ring a few more times while I swap records. Whoever it is can wait until I'm ready. Once Fleetwood Mac has started singing, I go downstairs in my bare feet to open the door. I don't wear socks. Not wearing socks makes me carefree and artsy. The installer from Bell has arrived. He carries a black rotary phone and some cables. I usher him upstairs, while Stevie Nicks launches into "Rhiannon." He fiddles with the cables for the rest of the album, but finally my phone comes to life. He hands me a slip of paper with my new phone number: 967-2111. Sounds good to me. I position my phone on top of the phone book and Yellow Pages the phone installer left for me. It's actually cool to have a vacant space with hardwood floors and a tall ceiling. It's my own private ballet studio. I perform a few jetés and execute an impeccable string of pirouettes back and forth across the room, before I curtsy to the audience. It's kind of a shame I need furniture.

Now that I have a phone, I can call the time-of-day number to find out how long I've been waiting for my delivery. "One forty-five," the time lady says. "One fifty-five," the time lady says. "Two oh eight," the time lady says.

"Rhiaaaaannon," Stevie Nicks says.

"Three thirty-three," the time lady says. Wow. I should win something for that one. "Three forty-five," the time lady says. "Four oh four," the time lady says. My doorbell rings. My couch is here. I get up awkwardly from the floor, shaking the pins and needles out of my legs. My stomach reminds me I didn't eat lunch. I go down and open the door to a torrential downpour. The delivery guys do not look happy as they lean my couch against Mr. Behrens's flocked wallpaper.

The first guy looks up the stairway and says, "No way that thing's getting up there."

The second guy looks up the stairway and says, "No way that thing's getting up there."

I mention I paid for delivery. Nobody asked me whether I had stairs. Or two landings. Or a Victorian house. The delivery guys sigh deeply, bend down, and dead-lift the couch. I go up the stairs ahead of them to open my door. I sit back down on the floor next to the phone, flip the records over, and phone the time lady. "Four thirty-five," she says. I look down the stairwell. The delivery guys are sitting on the second landing. Having a smoke. Several people who apparently live on my floor or above are milling about in the open area at the bottom of the stairs, which are completely blocked by my couch. "What's going on here?" one of them says. "What kind of idiot buys a couch that big when you live in a house like this?" I walk backward, out of view, into my apartment. Best not call attention to myself as that kind of idiot.

The time lady says, "Five oh two." I sit on the floor and turn the records yet again. Maybe I should get used to this not-having-furniture thing. "Five forty-three," the time lady says. There's a bunch of grunting, a crash, and a knock at my door. My couch is sitting on its left arm. The plastic that was covering the new upholstery is as shredded as the Pentagon Papers. I hustle the delivery guys through the door quickly so the unruly mob behind them doesn't see me. They flop the couch down in my living-bedroom then plop themselves down in their muddy jeans, looking at me expectantly. That's when I remember I have some beer in the fridge. I open two and hand them to the guys. They drain the bottles in three seconds and stay right where they are, although one of them makes a big show of checking his watch. Oh. I rummage through my backpack and find a crumpled ten-dollar bill. I hope that's enough because they know where I live.

I remove the remains of the plastic wrap from my new couch. Clumps of dried mud adhere to most of the cushions. Maybe beige was not the best idea. I pick at one of the clumps with my fingernail until it comes off and falls on the floor, scattering dirt into the middle of the room. Though. I start making a shopping list. My new phone rings. My first phone call! But who could be calling me? Nobody knows my number yet. But wait, the time lady probably knows my number. We're practically related. I lift the receiver expectantly.

"I'd like a large pepperoni, two Cokes, and a dozen chicken wings," the person on the other end says.

"Wrong number," I say. And hang up. Two minutes later the phone rings again.

A woman says, "Can I get two large, one with sausage on one half, ham on the other half, pineapple, green peppers, and extra cheese. One with just sauce and cheese. And onions."

"Wrong number," I say. And hang up. The phone rings again. I let it go for a dozen times, my hand hovering over the receiver, but I finally pick up. Could be a guy calling.

"I'd like a medium with black olives, onions, and spicy sausage. Double sauce," my caller says.

"Sure," I say. "Thirty minutes." I turn off the ringer on my phone. I'll deal with this tomorrow. Too bad. That phone number was kind of easy to remember. I fold out my new bed, make it with brand-new sheets that do not smell like dorm-room bleach, and settle in to spend my first night in my perfect apartment.

* * *

Frank is from Trinidad. Every word that comes out of his mouth sounds like he's gently wafting Caribbean waves toward the shore. I fight as hard as I can to not fall asleep on the beach. But I'm not on the beach. Frank is teaching me my new job at Dataline. I am the new Frank. I'd better pay attention.

"Okay," says Frank. "First you print out the form. One for each computer. Then you fill it out and file it in the binder. Then you go into the terminal room and start the process. And I am about to reveal the process to you, if you can snatch the pebble from my hands." He laughs like this is the funniest thing he has ever said. I totally get it. Sort of. But I'm a little confused about the paper form. I thought this was a computer company. Paperless office. That kind of stuff.

The room where the magic of my job happens is a ten-by-ten windowless place where old office furniture goes to die. Everyone calls it "the bridge" because of the vinyl office chair that used to have a back, which the guys think looks like Captain Kirk's throne. That's the chair positioned in front of the operator terminal that sits on a low metal table. It has a keyboard but no screen, just a roll of computer paper that feeds up from a box on the floor. Don told me I am one of a handful of people with access to the God login ID, which is 1,2. The password for this gets changed randomly plus every time an operator departs the company, voluntarily or involuntarily. Also, the password can only be transmitted verbally, from the mouth of the director of the computer room to authorized need-to-know ears. It is forbidden to write the password down. "When you play God, you can unleash a swarm of locusts just as easily as create a Garden of Eden," Don said to me yesterday. "You've got the whole world in your hands."

I look over Frank's shoulder as he types instructions into the computer terminal for the operators in the computer room on the third floor. He starts with the third computer, DA3. This seems a little illogical to me. How can he keep track of where he is if he starts in the middle? But I keep that thought to myself. He tears the printout off at the seam, hands it to me, and motions toward Captain Kirk's perch. I take it this means it's time for me to give it a try. I sit down and immediately pitch backward.

"Oh, the recline thing is kind of broken too," says Frank. I manage to achieve a facsimile of equilibrium and move the chair forward so I can reach the keyboard, which causes my knees to hit a ragged metal bar that supports the underside of the desk. I slide the chair back to survey the damage. My nylons are a mass of runs and blood trickles down both shins. Frank looks alarmed.

Crap. I cannot afford to damage my legs. I'm taking a ballet exam in a week. "Just a flesh wound," I say. That's why Frank was sitting with his knees spread so far apart. Or maybe that's just how guys sit. I'll either have to start wearing pants or keep several dozen pairs of pantyhose in my desk drawer. Or buy some goalie pads.

*   *   *

Mr. Bill comes up and looms over my cubicle after I arrive in the office on Tuesday morning. Mr. Bill is six feet five, a foot taller than me, and, it appears, two and a half times my body weight. Although we don't have a dress code per se, Mr. Bill colours way outside the lines. He wears plaid flannel shirts, faded dad jeans, and cowboy boots that look like he's stepped in horse manure a few too many times. He wears his signature outfit regardless of season. Mr. Bill is the head software guru. His name is, in fact, Bill, but the programmers call him Mr. Bill after the clay figurine character on *Saturday Night Live* that suffers indignities by Mr. Hands. However, in this case, it's Mr. Bill that inflicts the indignities. "Ooooooooooooooooh nooooooo! It's Mr. Bill," is the cry that goes up in the programming pen whenever he's in proximity, or actually, whenever he's within five miles of the building. Mr. Bill does not suffer bad coding gladly.

"FORLIB had to be recompiled," Bill says. "I need you to load it on all the computers before lunch." It's already ten thirty.

FORLIB is the Fortran subroutine library, I know that much. I don't really know exactly what it's for, but if Mr. Bill is asking, it must be important. I tell him I'll get right on it and head to the operator console room. I assume Captain Kirk's position. The chair teeters back and forth and once again pitches me into the metal bar under the desk. Another pair of pantyhose bites the dust. At least the fat scabs on my knees offer some protection from further harm. This remnant chair clearly has special powers. Otherwise, why would the guys put up with it? I turn on the terminal and log in to 1,2. *Invalid password*, it says. I try again. *Invalid password*. Just in case I spelled it wrong, I try once more. *You have violated maximum logins. You have violated console security*, the console printout says. This is not good. Not only did I lock myself out of 1,2, I also locked out everyone else. The operators won't be able to do their work, which means the computers won't work, which means our customers can't access their software. Or something like that. I need to find Alan, keeper of 1,2.

    I knock on Alan's door. Alan is partial to pastel polo shirts with golf club logos and wears a circular keychain with about a hundred keys on it attached to his belt loop. Like a jailer. He is always on the phone, barking orders to the operators upstairs. He waves me in as he continues to shout into the receiver, "Some idiot locked us out of 1,2! We only just changed the password an hour ago when we walked Evan out the door." Well that explains why my password didn't work.

    I tell Alan that Bill needs FORLIB updated right away and I wanted to check and see if the 1,2 password has changed before I try to login. The best defence is a good offence.

    Alan scowls at me. "There was a new password," he says. "And now there's going to be another one. Like I have all day to spend updating passwords." He turns to his terminal and bashes at the keyboard with his forefingers.

    "The new password is Dumbchick," he says. "Capital *D*." No need to take it out on me. He's the one who didn't tell me the password had changed. This place is full of unexploded landmines left over from some war I wasn't told about.

I walk the shreds of my pantyhose back to the console room and get to work. I log in successfully and start the process of sending the computer room the instructions for loading Bill's software and updating the index on each of the six computers. One good thing about DEC computers is the commands are all regular, normal English. *Print* means print. *Save* means save. *Mount* means mount.

Bill's software updates are stored on a tape up in the computer room. My job is to tell the operators what to do with it. *Mount tape FL10543 on DA1*, my fingers tell them. *Load tape FL10543 onto DA1*. Then I wait until the confirmation shows up on my console printout before I type *Dismount tape FL10543 from DA1*. I've got this, Frank. But unlike Frank's, my fingers fly over the keyboard instead of hunting and pecking. And away I go, in sequence, telling the operators to mount and dismount the tape on the remaining five computers: DA2, DA3, DA4, DA5, and DA6.

I head upstairs to the output window to retrieve the new FORLIB printout. The output window is at the top of the back staircase. It has a Formica counter ledge below a frosted window that slides open after I hit the bell that sits on the counter. I tell the operator I am collecting my printout, which is a stack of eleven-by-seventeen-inch paper as thick as the New York phone book. He starts to slide it across the ledge, then stops. "Are you a new secretary?"

"No," I say, "I'm the new Frank."

"You're much better looking than Frank," he says.

He's right. I am better looking than Frank. He's also right that most women here, other than in the training department, are secretaries. I'm glad I have a guy's job. I refuse to be stuck in a girl's job and get no respect. Except somehow, I'm still wearing skirts instead of pants, like back in high school when the boys could wear jeans but girls couldn't even wear tasteful trousers. Even though I have no principal telling me what to do, I'm reluctant to challenge the status quo. I'll wait until I'm sure I won't get fired.

I am wrestling the printout into its binder when Frank shows up in the console room. He tells me Alan wants to see me. Right away. Alan is on the phone when I get to his office, only this time he hangs up when he sees me. He tells me to come in and close the door. This sounds serious. Maybe he got in trouble for the new password.

Alan stands up and goes to the blackboard on his side wall. "Have you ever been in the computer room?" he asks. Of course I have never been in the computer room. Nobody's allowed in the computer room. But I guess that was a rhetorical question because he goes on, "The room is configured to maximize the amount of space between the computers so we can minimize the air conditioning." He picks up some chalk to draw a map showing where the computers are situated in the room. "DA2 is in the southwest corner because it was the first one we got. DA4 is a few feet east, and DA6 is all the way to the southeast. On the north side, we have DA5 in the corner, DA3 in the middle, and DA1 in the northeast corner."

I study the diagram for a minute or two. Geometry is not my strong suit, but even I can see what this means. I'm making them run a marathon every time I load software. After the operators mount and dismount a tape on DA1, they need to walk the entire diagonal length of the room to mount it on DA2. It's another trip across the room to continue to DA3. By the time they're finished doing my bidding, the operators have drawn a beautiful pentagram with their feet on the floor of the ten-thousand-square-foot room. Alan looks at me expectantly.

"Right," I say. "The computers are not lined up in numerical order, so if I ask tapes to be mounted in numerical sequence the operators have to do more work. Thanks for letting me know." No doubt there are more boobytraps lurking in the kingdom of the DEC10s.

3

Ditched

<u>1979</u>

My library room is a five-by-eight-foot space lined with shelves crammed tightly with technical specifications for hardware, softcover programming manuals, and computer-paper binders full of programming code. There are hardware manuals, software manuals, programming textbooks, and books that seem to be about computers in general. I pick up Tracy Kidder's *The Soul of a New Machine*. It opens at page sixty-seven. "Increasingly, computers communicate with other computers across vast distances. Banks store their money in computer systems. Oil companies store their crown jewels, seismic information, in computerized data banks," it says. This is interesting. At Waterloo, nobody ever talked about how businesses use computers, only about scientific calculations and engineering equations. Maybe someday I'll learn more about this.

In the Dewey Decimal Classification system, computer science falls under 000. Computers did not exist in 1876 when Mr. Dewey invented it. Computer science snuck in sometime in the twentieth century and was relegated to the category already occupied by information and general works, the de facto junkpile for random stuff. Because what kind of library real estate could it possibly need?

If I had used the Dewey Decimal system to organize the books at Dataline, all my technical manuals and programming books would have sat on the shelf under 000.01. The upside of this would have been that when someone asked me to find the *PDP 10 Tape Library Manual*, all I would have needed to do is tell them to look under 000.01. The Library of Congress was no more prescient about the eventual arrival of computers. Computer science lives within science, relegated to the decidedly unroomy confines of QA76.75. That's why I decided the best approach was to create my own classification system. Besides, it's not like anybody here would know a Dewey decimal from a Huey or Louie decimal.

Five months after its creation, my library classification system is running as smoothly as a well-balanced DEC 10 tape drive. I have created a place where computer science can stretch its considerable tentacles. Hardware stuff sits together under *H* with additional letters indicating the type of manual. HTP for tape drives. There is also a sequential number starting at 1 to differentiate between the volumes. Same thing for software (*S*), programming (*P*), and general books (*G*). I also wrote a program to create a keyword-in-context index, so people who are allergic to classification systems can look books up by any word in the title or description. Someday soon, I'll be in the Library Hall of Fame. Just as soon as they invent one.

* * *

My library desk is wedged between the short wall and the door. The door is purely decorative: there is no way to close it, either inside or outside the room. Whenever I'm librarian-ing, I am in full view of anyone who walks by. This is a problem because the programming guys all treat me as an excuse for a coffee break. An endless stream of time-wasters invite themselves to lean against the door jamb and chat with the librarian about subjects that are only interesting to programming guys, like how fast they can solve a Rubik's Cube. This does not escape Mr. Bill's notice. He stands up, rests his elbows on the top of his cubicle, and bellows in the direction of the library, "Can any of you find time to fit a work break in between the coffee breaks?"

This is followed by a chorus of "Oooooh noooooo," as the programmers scatter back to their lair. I don't know if this results in a flurry of programming or not, but at least the librarian-ing can resume. For five minutes. Bob from sales spies an opening and takes it. Bob is nothing like the programmers, who specialize in ironic t-shirts that are never washed lest they wear out, track pants that have never seen the inside of a gym, and hair that finds the concept of a comb offensive. Bob looks like Tom Selleck, only blond. His double-breasted suit is as impeccable as his white monogrammed shirt and gold cufflinks that are probably real gold.

"Hi," he says. "I'm Bob. From sales. You're the librarian? Is this what librarians look like these days?"

If there is a suitable answer to this question, I don't know what it is, so all I say is "Hi." Bob's chitchat is a little more refined than what I endure from the programmers. The weather. The hockey scores. The new restaurant he wants to try.

Mr. Bill stands up again. "What have you sold lately, Bob?"

This comment slides right off the toes of Bob's shiny shoes. "Hey, Bill," he says. "You're cramping my style. I'm learning things I never knew about librarians."

This gets Don's attention. He's standing at Fenella's desk a few feet away from my library room. "Hands off my librarian," he says. Bob waves in Don's direction and saunters toward the sales corner, like that's what he was planning on doing all along. Soon, I will learn that Bob has a habit of getting what he wants.

* * *

The programmers have stopped their parade. I guess Mr. Bill followed up his bark with a bite. But Bob comes by every day at ten and three for the next two weeks to chat about the weather, the hockey scores, and the new restaurant he wants to try. While he chatters, I go about my business, putting printouts into binders, reshelving manuals, and dusting my desk. I do not want to get in trouble. Mr. Bill always seems to be lurking nearby.

I'm walking across the parking lot on Friday when I hear a *pssst* to my left. It's Bob. He looks over his shoulder, as if making sure nobody's within earshot, and says, "I have a reservation for tonight at that new restaurant. Want to go?"

As I weigh the option of a free meal against the allure of another night of Kraft Dinner, Don comes out the front door and heads to his car. "And I'd really like us to get some books about sales," Bob says loudly. "We can discuss on Monday." We both watch as Don waves and drives off. I decide a free meal with blond Tom Selleck would not be half bad, but I sense this is something we will need to keep to ourselves. I can just imagine what the operators would do with this information. I tell Bob to hang back for a minute. I walk across the parking lot to the road, then up the short block to the light at Davenport, where there's a dessert restaurant. That's how exotic Toronto is. There's a sit-down restaurant that only sells dessert. Bob's still standing in the parking lot. I wave at him, pointing in the direction of Bedford Road. He saunters casually to the opposite side of the intersection. The light changes and we walk toward my apartment. Bob stays on the left side of the street as I walk on the right. I feel like we should have a secret password, like the spies in *Get Smart*. *The moon is full*, I'll shout across the road. *But only on Tuesdays*, Bob will reply. Then we'll exchange secret documents. Or books about how to sell computer stuff.

Bob arrives at my porch just as I am unlocking the front door. I tell him to follow me upstairs. Then I hear what I just said. I sound like I own a bordello. Bob does not seem concerned. I open my apartment and tell him to have a seat while I put my stuff away and change my shoes. Librarian pumps are not the thing to wear to a fancy restaurant. I swap into black wet-look, sling-back, spike-heel disco shoes and sit down beside him on the couch. "How about this weather?" I say. "Pretty warm for September. How about those Leafs? All the way, this year, for sure. Tell me more about the restaurant." I cannot get myself to shut up nor say anything sensible. I have a guy who looks like he could be on the cover of *Esquire* sitting right next to me.

Bob snakes his arm across the top of the couch behind my neck, leans in, and kisses me. "I've been wanting to do that for weeks," he says. "I was expecting one of the programmers to beat me to it." Seriously? Is that why the programmers were hanging around? Am I an idiot? *Yes*, my inside voice answers itself. *You are a complete idiot*. A complete idiot who is somehow now making out with Bob. After an indecent interval, Bob looks at his watch. "Reservation's at seven. We'd better get going," he says. As if it's my fault we're going to be late.

The restaurant maître d' greets Bob like an old friend and leads us to a velvet banquette in the corner. So much for this being a restaurant he wanted to try. He's clearly tried it a zillion times, probably with a zillion women. The candlelight barely illuminates the menu. "I'll order for us," says Bob. What is this? A James Bond movie? Bob and the waiter discuss wine vintages and what would go best with the chateaubriand for two. "And Caesar salad to start," says Bob. "The chocolate soufflé for dessert." The waiter returns with two flutes of champagne and a bottle of something dusty. "You'd better get used to this," says Bob. Not a chance. I would never want this to be less than special.

As we eat, we talk about work and Mr. Bill and the programmers and the timesharing business and whether Gerry, the sales VP, is sleeping with his secretary. Bob tells me he used to play hockey and broke his nose so many times he had to get a nose job. I tell him about growing up in Deep River and ballet and not really being convinced I want to be a librarian. Even the computer kind. Bob says that surely I didn't want to miss the chance to single-handedly change the librarian stereotype. He may have a point there.

We close down the restaurant and take a cab back to my place. Bob tells the driver to wait while he walks me to my door, where he kisses me goodnight. "I'll see you tomorrow night. And the night after that. And the night after that," he says. "You can't get rid of me."

* * *

1980

"I have some news," Bob tells me. "I'm getting promoted. I'm going to open up a Dataline office in Calgary." Well, that certainly counts as news. "We've got someone scouting out the space right now, but it won't be until March before I'll have to move out there." Okay, easy come, easy go. But that's not really how I feel. I finally have a boyfriend. A good-looking boyfriend. A boyfriend who thinks I'm a catch. This is not the ending I had in mind.

Bob and I wander the neighbourhood on Sunday after breakfast. We walk past the Audi dealer and he shows me a car like the one he just bought. "Let's drive it out to Calgary together when it gets delivered," he says. I tell him I don't drive, long story, you don't want to know. "No problem. I can drive the whole way," Bob says. "Just keep me company." I ask Bob how long he thinks it'll take. "Three days, at most. Then you can hang out in Calgary for a few days and I'll pay for your flight back," he says. I have enough vacation to take a week off. Sounds like a good adventure. Also sounds like Bob's not dumping me yet.

In early March the snow is melting fast, and it's warm enough that I only need to wear the Cowichan sweater I bought in Victoria. It's like one of those curling sweaters with the zipper up front, except it has dolphins on it instead of curling rocks. When Bob swings by to pick me up in his brand-new car early on a Saturday morning, I debate whether to bring gloves and a scarf, but it's spring. It can only get warmer. We are going to drive north to the Trans-Canada, around Lake Superior, through Winnipeg and Regina, and end up in Calgary. Not the U.S. way. It will take twenty-four hours just to get out of Ontario and another fourteen from there.

"I bought some tapes so we'll have something to listen to. The radio signal usually craps out after Sudbury," says Bob.

I open the latch of the glove compartment and pull out *Running on Empty*. I hope that Jackson Browne is not clairvoyant. I rummage around some more and retrieve *Hasten Down the Wind*. Linda Ronstadt is sounding a little ominous too. "Is this a joke, Bob?" I say. He doesn't answer. He's too busy trying to figure out how the windshield wipers work. We'll listen to the radio for now.

"We can stop for lunch in Parry Sound," Bob says. "We'll know we're getting close when we see the big billboard that says 'Home of Bobby Orr.'"

"Bobby Orr's from Parry Sound?" I say. "I don't believe it. You're making that up. Bobby Orr's from Boston."

"Okay, I'll bet you," says Bob. "If there's a Bobby Orr sign, you're buying lunch."

There'd better not be a Bobby Orr billboard. I just realized I forgot to go to the bank. I have about a buck in change on me. I figured Bob was going to pay for everything, since the company's covering his expenses for the trip. We motor on up Highway 69 toward the turnoff for the Trans-Canada. "See! Right there. Home of Bobby Orr," Bob says, with a little too much enthusiasm. "I'm going to get a steak sandwich with extra fries. Nothing like a free lunch." He turns off the highway into Parry Sound and parks behind a roadhouse pub.

We walk into the restaurant and the hostess says, "Bob! Where have you been?" Bob grins, introduces me, and heads to a booth in the back.

"Bob," I say. "Have we been getting free meals everywhere we go? Even at that fancy restaurant in Yorkville?"

Bob looks pleased with himself. "Go ahead. Order anything on the menu," he says. "It's on me."

*　*　*

As promised, the radio switches to solid static once we are on the way toward Sudbury. I load Jackson Browne into the tape deck. It's great road-trip music. By the fourth time through, we know all the words. And by the fifth time, it starts to snow. Big wet flakes. It's still snowing when we get to Thunder Bay. Snowing and dark. But Bob wants to keep driving. So we do. Linda Ronstadt takes over jukebox duty and we press on. About an hour out of Thunder Bay, the highway is covered in half a foot of snow, which is also blowing sideways across the road. The sign up ahead says Ignace, Population 1,200. I can see what looks like a motel sign just off the highway. The kind of motel sign that used to have five letters but is now down to three and proudly announces it is fully equipped with black-and-white TV.

"I think we should stop, Bob," I say. He reluctantly agrees.

"Never thought I'd ever get to spend the night in Ignace," he says. "Hope they have some food. I'll probably have to pay for it, though."

There is only food in Ignace if you count vending-machine food as food. We buy some Coke and some salt-and-vinegar chips and crash in the finest room of the finest motel Ignace has to offer. We leave just after dawn. Bob has to fold up a newspaper to scrape the snow off the car because we have no winter accoutrements. My gloveless hands are freezing. We continue heading west. "When we cross into Manitoba, I'm going to give you a great big kiss," Bob says. Linda Ronstadt resumes her umpteenth rendition of "That'll Be the Day (That I Die)." Really, Linda? I think we should revert to "Running on Empty" because we're also doing a pretty good job of that. I, too, will be glad to see the back end of Ontario.

There it is, just up ahead. A sign that says "Welcome to Manitoba." Bob hoots, leans over, takes his hands off the wheel, and kisses me. Immediately, the car swerves to the left and flies into the wide ditch that acts as the median. Good thing Manitoba specializes in wide-open spaces, otherwise we'd be in the oncoming lane. And good thing it's just past nine in the morning instead of nine at night. We slide a few yards, plowing the snow into a mound with the front bumper before we stop. We sit in silence for ten minutes, contemplating the snow drift on the windshield. I look over at Bob. "I guess it's the thought that counts," I say.

Bob gets out of the car to assess the damage, sinking up to his knees in the snow. Wearing dress shoes may not have been the best idea. At this moment, I realize nobody knows where I am, I have no ID on me, and I have no money. If I die in this ditch I will not be the subject of a nationwide search, until a month from now when Mr. Behrens notices I've stopped paying rent. "I'm going to check and see how deep the front wheels are sunk," says Bob. "Can you put your foot on the brake?" I slide over to the driver's seat and look down at the pedals. I have never been behind the steering wheel of a car. I have no idea which one is the brake. I didn't even pass the written driver's test. I am not going to ask Bob, though. He'll think I'm a moron. I just go with the one on the right. The front wheels spin, kicking snow into Bob's face. "The brake! The brake!" Bob shouts. Okay. Wrong choice. But at least I've proven we're not permanently stuck. Bob wipes the snow off his forehead with the sleeve of his jacket, gets back in the car, and tuns on the hazard lights.

We wait an hour in Manitoba March, a delightful time of year that approximates Toronto January, until a farmer in a pickup truck stops by the side of the road. He motions for us to roll down the window. "You happy in that ditch or do you need help?" he says. Bob gets out and wades through the snow to the edge of the highway. I can see him conferring with the farmer. Bob waves at me to join him. I leap from footprint to footprint to minimize the inevitable snow soakers. The farmer tells me to wait in the cab of the truck and hands Bob a pair of rubber boots. He hefts a length of chain and attaches it to a pull-bar on the back of the truck while Bob takes the other end to the car. The farmer gets us out first try. I guess he does this a lot. Bob thanks him profusely. The farmer mutters under his breath about city slickers and fancy cars. Disaster averted. Turns out though, going off the road in Manitoba was not the worst of our problems. Or to be correct, the worst of my problems.

It's almost midnight when we get to Calgary and we've been on the road for three days solid. Bob already has an apartment that the company has furnished for him. I throw my satchel into the bedroom, brush my teeth, and flop down on the bed. Bob's fancy Calgary bedroom has a waterbed with a built-in bookcase in the cannonball headboard. The heated water is kind of nice but makes me constantly want to pee. The thing about waterbeds is you are at the mercy of the weight and movement of the weightier person in the bed. Which would be Bob. As he is lulled to sleep by his buoyancy, I pitch and roll like I'm in a lifeboat launched from the Titanic, with no hope of reaching land.

Bob neglected to tell me he has a roommate, Andy, who is also relocating from the Toronto office. Andy greets me in the morning when I wander into the kitchen in a t-shirt and underwear to see if there's any tea. "So, you and Bob," he says, leering in my direction. "I guess the programmers are a little upset."

Bob hears my shriek, rousts himself from the water-womb, and comes into the kitchen to investigate. He tells Andy to smarten up and go out and pick us up some breakfast. I steal back to the bedroom, pull my jeans on, shrug into a fresh t-shirt, and comb my hair with my fingers. I didn't bring a comb either. My notion of a road trip was more like *Roman Holiday* than *National Lampoon's Vacation*.

Andy and Bob are drinking coffee from paper Tim Hortons cups and eating chocolate-glazed doughnuts when I come back into the kitchen. Bob hands me a tea and a sour-cream glazed. Then the phone rings. It's the Dataline operations room in Toronto. "Hey," says Andy. "You won't believe who's here in Calgary with me and Bob!"

Bob reaches over, slaps the phone out of Andy's hand, and hangs it up. "They'll call back," Bob says. "And when they do, tell them you just saw Bobby Orr at the coffee shop. And by the way, you're buying the coffee for a year, minimum."

Why would the operations room be calling Andy? I don't think Andy can be trusted. Do they know something already? This is not good.

* * *

Mr. Bill's waiting for me in my cubicle with his boots up on my desk when I get back to the office on Monday. "How was your vacation?" he asks. This is odd. Mr. Bill has never cared about my vacation plans before. "I'm going to rebuild the Fortran subroutine library today. Bob needs it updated before we go live in Calgary."

"Good to know," I say. "I'll install it when you're done."

Bill gets up from my chair and ambles off toward the console room. "The operators are restless today," he says as he's leaving. "They must have a juicy bit of info." Andy blabbed. I know it. But I don't exactly know what Bill knows.

On Tuesday, Bill's camped in my cubicle again. "Got a call from Bob yesterday," he says. "Bob thinks I ought to send you out to Calgary to get their software organized. Do you know why Bob would want you to do that? Do you think I should help Bob out?" By my count, Bill has said "Bob" a thousand times in ten seconds.

I tell Bill I have no idea and that I have lots to do, so could he please get out of my office? He smirks and slowly extracts himself from my chair. In two hours, when the workday starts in Calgary, I call Bob on the no-toll bridge line so nobody will know that I called. "Bob, did you ask Bill to send me out? What the hell?"

Bob laughs. Easy for him. Bob is safe as the wonder boy who's expanding the company. I'm the one who'll end up with the bad reputation. The girl librarian who sleeps around with the management.

I don't hear from Bob for the next four months. Opening the new office must be keeping him too busy to think about Toronto girlfriends. Then, on a random day in August, I get a call on the bridge line. From Bob. "Hi," he says with supreme eloquence. "Guess what? I'm getting married." He must be joking. I tell him I'm getting married too. "No, really. I'm getting married," he says. "I thought you should know before the operators do their thing."

Bill walks by just as I hang up and leans over the top of my cubicle. "Hey, the operators say Bob's getting married. I guess he'll be wanting me to send you out to help with the wedding!" He snorts and ambles off toward the programming corral.

I tell Bill to shut up (with my inside voice) then I go into the console room to load a new batch of software. I make sure to do this in precise numerical order. In quick succession. *Mount on DA1. Mount on DA2. Mount on DA3. Mount on DA4. Mount on DA5. Mount on DA6.* I smile as I envision the operators swearing and scurrying around upstairs.

4

Knock Three Times on the Ceiling

1980

There's somebody sorting through the mail that's sitting on the shelf on top of the radiator in the front hall of 120 Bedford Road when I get home from work. He looks up when I come through the door, then looks back at the mail. He holds up a fan of letters, as if he is a magician asking me to pick a card. One of them is indeed mine. "Marilyn," he says, as I take my letter out of the middle of his mail bouquet. Clearly, he's memorized the names on the letters. "Nice to meet you. I'm Morris." He puts the rest of the letters back on the shelf, looks at my suit and briefcase and says, "So you're the businesswoman I see walking to work every morning. I always wondered who you were."

Morris has an aquiline nose and a sleek dark beard. His hair is early-eighties long, slicked straight back from his forehead, brushing the collar of his open-neck white dress shirt; a puka-shell necklace nestles close to his clavicle. His shirt is tucked into a pair of fancy jeans. He follows me up the stairs. "This is me," I say, when we get to the second floor. I fumble with my key, drop it, pick it up, drop it again. So much for an unflappable working girl. "Come for a drink later tonight," he says. "Give me your number and I'll call you." I rhyme off my digits, pick my key up from the floor, and trip over my briefcase as I enter my apartment.

    I'm watching a rerun of *The Mary Tyler Moore Show* after dinner when the phone rings. I pick it up and hear dead air. It rings again. Dead air again. This goes on for several hundred more times. There's a knock on the door. It's Morris. "I think there's a problem with your phone," he says. "Come on up to my place, if you like." His apartment is on the third floor, with a slanted ceiling and a triangular-shaped window nestled in below the eaves. He has divided his main room into living and sleeping areas, separated by a beaded curtain. His couch is covered with an Indian bedspread and his lampshades are draped with red chiffon scarves. There's a shark's jawbone on the Turkish trunk that serves as his coffee table. It's the exact opposite of my monochromatic Scandinavian taste. If I had to put a name to it, I'd call his style bachelor bordello. I wonder what this guy does for a living. Something artsy, probably.

    Morris goes into the kitchen and returns with a bottle of red wine and two jelly glasses, one decorated with Fred Flintstone and the other with Betty Rubble. "He's wife swapping," says Morris. I'm guessing he thinks this is clever. He probably deliberately chose those two glasses. We clink Fred and Betty and sit on the couch. "What do you do after you leave every morning with that briefcase? I like that grey skirt you wear, by the way." I describe the timesharing industry and my job as custodian of the software on the DEC 10s, all the while thinking there's something a little creepy about a guy who spies on me from the third-floor window when I leave the house. I prattle on about Mr. Bill and all the guys I work with.

"Do you date any of those guys?" he asks.

"I guess you've never met a programmer," I say. "Otherwise you wouldn't have asked that question." I neglect to mention Bob. It's time to change the subject. "What about you?"

"Do I date guys?" Morris says. "Only sometimes." He says this with a poker face, so I have no idea whether this is supposed to be a joke or not, until he laughs. "Damn I'm good. I've been practising controlling my expression. I'm going to be a litigator." Turns out Morris is a newly minted lawyer, getting ready for the bar exam. "I was almost a lawyer," I say. "What was your LSAT score?" he asks. I tell him and he looks at me, showing no reaction. Better than his, I bet.

* * *

1976

My clock radio clicks on at six in the morning. Six on a Saturday morning, at the University of Waterloo. Gary Wright is singing about dreams. If only I was still dreaming. There is serious business ahead. I gather my morning grooming stuff and make my way down the hall to the bathroom, which is completely empty. A good thing. I go into a stall to pee while I brush my teeth. No time to spare. The wall of the toilet enclosure is covered in butcher paper and has the nub of a red crayon attached at the top with a piece of string, so you can add to the noninvasive graffiti. The theme is a riff on "Fifty Ways to Leave Your Lover," Paul Simon's song du jour. But we aren't as clever as he is. *Fall off a cliff, Cliff. Have a nice day, Ray. You're dead to me, Fred. Why didn't you take me on that trip to Florida? And besides, who was that girl I saw you with at the campus pub last week, you asshole Tim!*

I return to my room, locate a pair of overalls that are almost clean, wrap a purple handkerchief bandana around my unwashed hair, and head out the door to the Waterloo Physical Activity Centre (a.k.a. the gym). It's so early that I pass people straggling home from the night before. The meal hall isn't even open yet.

It's Law School admission test day. I figure I'll get there in time to choose a good spot, arrange my pencils and eraser, and relax before the test. Apparently, everyone else had the same idea because the corridor outside the main gym is packed with test-takers. There's a table set up by the door but nobody's there yet to sign us into the room. I look around to see who's showed up. I recognize a couple of guys from my Poli Sci class but don't see anyone else I know. I have my Ronald McDonald plastic, zippered pencil case, containing the approved HB pencils, a pink eraser, a small pencil sharpener, a compass, and a protractor. I don't think I'll need the compass or protractor, at least I dearly hope not, but they live in the pencil case and I didn't want to evict them. The Ronald McDonald theme is meant to be ironic. No clowns allowed in a group of wannabe lawyers. Most people are clutching an *LSAT Preparation* book, cramming up until the last minute. I did borrow one from the library a few weeks ago, but the test is multiple choice, or as we all call it, multiple guess. No need to memorize answers.

Finally, at quarter to eight, a woman wearing sensible shoes and thick glasses shows up with bundles of test sheets, and sits down at the check-in table. "I need to see your student ID card and I need you to sign the sheet. Your signature must match your ID exactly," she says. "And leave all bags at the door." This is before photo student ID was considered a good idea. The only official photo of me on university property is on the card that gets me into the meal hall. So theoretically, anyone who's a good forger could write someone else's LSAT test. I'm a little confused by this notion because anyone attempting to do an end run around the application credentials would land in a pile of quicksand when they showed up at law school. I'd rather take the straight and narrow route. Besides, both my grandfathers are lawyers, and even if they're lawyers in Québec's wonky legal system, with French-from-France civil law, I hope some of their legal DNA lurks in my veins. Or even more hopefully, lurks in my brain. If I don't become a lawyer, I have decided I will become a librarian. I like books. It could be a good gig. Maybe.

 The test question booklet is thirty pages divided into six timed sections of thirty-five minutes each. I'll be stuck in this chair for four hours. Except we do get two breaks toward the end, probably so the gym janitors can mop up the puddles of pee. The first section is analytical reasoning. Exactly like I've been learning in philosophy classes. Stuff like: "Harold is a grandfather. Harold is bald. Therefore, all grandfathers are bald." I can do this. Next up: logical reasoning. This is fantastic. I've taken five logic courses so far. Finally, reading comprehension. Well really, if I can comprehend a convoluted Dickens storyline, I can comprehend anything. Maybe philosophy is useful after all.

* * *

1980

After a particularly successful rebuild of the world (a.k.a. the Fortran subroutine library) Bill offers to take me out to lunch. "I invited a few of the guys," he says. We take Rodney's car, a light blue BMW 2002 that looks more like a Datsun than a fancy foreign automobile. Bill crams himself and his cowboy boots into the back seat beside Ray from sales, looking like he's the main event at a Shriner's circus. Rodney opens the front passenger door for me and holds it long enough so he can grab a good view of my legs as I manoeuvre into Germany's idea of an appropriate bucket seat: so low it's practically camped out on Don's precious parking lot pavement. My skirt was definitely not designed for this. The tweedy raw silk is elegant and ends sensibly enough at mid-calf, but there's a slit up the front that ends way north of my knees. Once again, ease of walking is no match for ease of sitting.

We drive down to Bloor, then head west past Spadina, ending up at a block that's strangely infested with Hungarian restaurants. We enter a blue door, which takes us through a long dark corridor that smells like cabbage. It opens up into a tiny restaurant called the Blue Cellar Room. Waitresses with beefy arms wearing vaguely Germanic blue and white waitress dresses heft trays filled with schnitzels that are bigger than my head. Looks like Bill has joined the bandwagon of people trying to fatten me up.

Bill springs for a carafe of house wine to celebrate. It's as rough and tannic as the plonky Szekszardi Voros we used to drink at university. Two bucks a liter. Good at cutting grease, though, which is appropriate since there doesn't seem to be anything other than schnitzel on the menu. No need to spend a lot of time deciding what to order. Rodney looks at me and says, "You know that guy Peter Demeter who hired someone to murder his wife? This is where he met the hitman. Need anyone taken out? A few operators maybe? We'll never tell." The guys all laugh like Rodney's the next John Candy. I hope no operators actually eat here. It might give them ideas. Maybe I should dial down my reign of feverish tape-mounting computer room footwork.

The topic of lunch conversation, after we exhaust the mechanics of hiring a hitman, is, as usual, me. Did I go to Bob's wedding? Who am I dating? Doctors and lawyers, I tell them. It's sort of true. I could be going out with a lawyer soon. I tell them I wouldn't touch a computer programmer with a thirty-foot pole.

* * *

Karen and I are out for brunch at Toby's Good Eats, sitting in a green vinyl booth, eating sunshine salads instead of burgers. Sprouts, chicken breast, avocado, strawberries. Very exotic. She's been my friend since middle school in Deep River, when the kids from both sides of town converged in Grade 7. We've both achieved our goal of fleeing our small town for the city lights where we can finally be anonymous, but we still hang out together, tethered by the shared experience of our weird scientific-company town. "His name is what?" she says. "Like the cat? You're dating a cat?" I'm talking about Morris. "That is hilarious. I decree The Cat is now officially his name." I tell her he's good looking but a little weird, but maybe all lawyers are weird.

"We're going to the Paradise theatre tonight to see that Jeanne Moreau movie, *L'adolescente*. He seems to like foreign films. It's the third one we've been to in five days," I say.

Karen tells me she thinks he sounds more pretentious than weird. "You've never seen his apartment," I say.

"Wait a minute. You've been out with him three times this week already?" Karen is incredulous. "A pretentious weirdo with a goofy name? You must be desperate."

"Remember that guy Brian you were seeing? The one who wouldn't give you his phone number and kept a change of clothes in the back seat of his Jaguar?" At least I don't date drug dealing stockbrokers. Lawyers are usually on the right side of the law. There must be thousands of eligible guys in Toronto and yet they are as elusive as a seat on the subway in rush hour.

I'm at home getting ready for my date when the phone rings. It's The Cat, saying he can't go to the movies tonight. He has to study for the bar exam. He hangs up quickly, before I can reply. I call Karen right away. "Well, now you can't say I'm seeing him too much. The Cat just bailed." I'm not going to sit in my apartment by myself on a Saturday night. I convince Karen to go out to Grossman's with me. Morgan Davis is playing.

We get off the College streetcar at Spadina and walk a few blocks south. Grossman's was brand spanking new in 1943, and the owner prefers to keep it in vintage condition. The asbestos-tile floor shows vestiges of blue underneath the grime, and the walls that were probably beige at one point are now the colour of nicotine. This is a place where you avoid visiting the bathroom. This is a place you go to hear raunchy blues. Karen and I snag a wobbly table at the back and order the only thing available: no name draft. I look around while the band is getting set up. My idle gaze snags on something that looks familiar. Holy crap! The Cat is sitting near the front. With a girl. I poke Karen. "It's The Cat! Over there! Chatting with Morgan Davis. He's with a girl!"

Karen turns to look in the direction I'm pointing. "He's very attractive," she says. "Not in Bob's league, but not bad at all. The girl's pretty hot too. I wonder how she got her Calvin's so tight?" I tell her we have to leave. Now. I can't be in the same room with him and some skanky girl. Some skanky girl he ditched me for. And furthermore, I will never speak to him again. Karen and I leave some change on the table for the untouched drinks and head for the door. The usual rowdy crowd is on the Spadina 77 bus, all of them going out as we head home. Another wasted Saturday night. Karen and I part company at the subway. It's only one stop to St. George so I might as well walk. I stomp and swear my way to Bedford Road. No rapist would dare mess with me. I look up at The Cat's window. There's a faint glow behind the curtain. I unlock my door and flop on my bed, which sits unmade and un-couched since the morning. I eye my phone. It couldn't hurt. I dial The Cat's number but hang up just before it hits his machine. I was going to say something like "Thought I'd give you a study break. I guess you've gone out for some fresh air." Or "All study and no play makes you a dull boy." Something original and clever. Something that hints I know he wasn't home studying. But what would be the point? I turn off my light.

At two in the morning my phone wakes me. I pick it up and hear nothing. It must be acting up again. But then I hear breathing. "Want to go out next week? I'm busy Saturday but we could do mid-week. I hope you didn't see that movie without me. I'm just going to bed now. Can't believe I studied so late." The Cat disconnects. At least technically I didn't speak to him.

* * *

Ruth's boyfriend, Steve, is in town for a business meeting. She's also a friend from Deep River, but she stayed in Waterloo. I take the bus there sometimes, to remind myself how much I hate taking the bus and how glad I am to be in Toronto. Ruth thinks she is in charge of putting meat on my bones, so she arranges for me to get a free meal as often as she can. "I gave Steve your number," she said when she called last week. "He has an expense account."

Steve calls me at work on Thursday and asks if I want to go for dinner and maybe somewhere after. He picks me up from Dataline in some kind of sports car. The sleek, low-to-the-ground kind with a manual transmission and a racing stripe. I'm not sure how he folds himself into it, since he's well over six feet. We're both wearing work clothes. His suit is navy blue and looks expensive. I have on my raw-silk skirt, the one with the slit that runs up the front, and a beige silk blouse with prodigious shoulder pads. My red heels are a little too high for walking more than a block or two. I usually wear my runners to work and change footwear at my desk. The nether regions of my cubicle look like the floor around the try-on benches at a shoe store. Another thing the programmers make fun of. I slide into Steve's bucket passenger seat, once again proving I'm not good at choosing skirts that behave themselves. He burns rubber out of the parking lot, just as Don is leaving the building. I squish down and pretend I'm pulling something out of my briefcase. Don will not be happy with those tire marks.

We lurch down Spadina as Steve floors it then piles on the brakes as the traffic slows for buses and jaywalkers. He parks and we take the stairs up to a fancy Chinese restaurant at Spadina and Dundas. This is one of the things that amazes me about Toronto: there are fancy Chinese restaurants, with tablecloths and chandeliers. Steve's been here before. He says Ruth really likes fancy-pants Chinese so he thought I would too. The menus are gigantic, gold-tasseled books with pages and pages of items. Mine has no prices, but I'm assuming his does. I have learned this is what the fancy restaurants do. He's paying, anyhow. Expense account. Steve orders for both of us. We're having Singapore Slings, the banquet for two, and some kind of wine that requires an extended consultation with the wine steward.

It's a leisurely meal of eight different courses with pauses in between. We are there for three hours. We chat about all kinds of stuff, like Steve's job at the University of Waterloo and how weird it is to be employed there instead of being a student. "The kids in the class call me 'sir,'" he says. We talk about foreign films, which luckily, I've gained an in-depth knowledge of lately, and music. I never knew he was into jazz and blues. I tell him about Morgan Davis, and that he's playing tonight at the El Mocambo, just up the street. "Let's go," he says. "I'd certainly never get to see him if I was with Ruth." I neglect to mention my hidden agenda. Chances are good The Cat will be there. I can waltz in with a handsome businessman and make him jealous.

The downstairs room of the El Mo is where most stuff happens, not the upstairs one where the Rolling Stones have played. It's your typical dingy bar, and has, for some reason, an old Woolworth's sign imbedded in the wall above the stage. It's hard to see for a few minutes until my eyes adjust to the gloom and clouds of secondhand smoke. Sure enough, there's The Cat sitting with some friends just up on the left. His friend Ben sees me first. He waves his arms. "Over here!" he says. "Hey, Morris, look who the cat dragged in. Ha ha ha. Sit with us." They are right beside one of the speakers. There are two spare seats. It would seem rude not to sit with them. I wouldn't want to be rude. Steve does not look too happy about sitting on the sticky bar chair in his fancy suit, but he does it anyway. When the waitress comes, Steve buys a round for everyone, slapping his platinum American Express card on top of the table to run a tab. Expense account.

Then the music starts, so we can't talk. I see The Cat eying Steve, but that doesn't stop him from drinking his free beer. The speaker is pounding, distorting the sound, but there's nowhere else to sit. Finally, the band takes a break. Steve leans over and cups his hands around my ear. "Let's get out of here," he says. "My ears are going to ring for the next week. And I doubt I'll ever get the smell of this place out of my clothes." We stand up, say goodbye to The Cat and the guys, and walk out. I'm certainly not going to turn around, but I'm sure The Cat is staring at my back. Or maybe I just hope he's staring at my back.

Steve pulls in to the mutual drive beside my apartment and turns the car off. I guess that's how manual transmissions work. Maybe they can't idle very long. I retrieve my briefcase, thank him for a lovely evening, and reach for the door handle. Steve leans across and kisses me. Not a "just friends" kiss. "Aren't you going to invite me in?" he says. "I paid for dinner and everything. It was over a hundred bucks. Not to mention the drinks I bought for those guys. Who were they anyway? That Morris guy was kind of creepy. I saw him looking at your legs. Not that they aren't fine legs. But you know what I mean. What kind of guy does that when it was clear we were on a date?" We were on a date? What kind of guy goes on a date with his girlfriend's best friend?

I am momentarily speechless, then my mouth springs into action. "My goodness, Steve," I say. "It's a work night. I have to be at the office by eight. Thanks for everything!" I scramble out of the seat, close the door, and run up the steps to the house as fast as my high heels will carry me. I unlock my apartment, dump my stuff, take off my shoes, and sit down on the couch. What am I going to tell Ruth? Am I going to tell Ruth? How is it that the guy I want to be my boyfriend only sort of wants to be my boyfriend, while my friend's boyfriend only sort of wants to be her boyfriend? My phone had better not ring at two in the morning. If it does there's no way I'm answering it. Probably.

5

Time Out

<u>1981</u>

In a rundown low-rise building on Queen Street West, up two flights of dusty wooden stairs bowed in the middle from thousands of footprints, through a metal exit door, there's a makeshift ballet studio. It reeks of ancient sweat, an aroma that reminds me of the boys' gym in high school. Apparently, contrary to popular belief, girls' sweat does not smell like rose petals. The changing facility is in a corner of the room, cordoned off with grubby sheets hanging from clothespins on a piece of wire that sags in the middle. I dump my dance bag on the floor near the wooden bench. Kim and Joanne are already here, tying up their ribbons.

    I liberate my tights, leotard, and legwarmers from my bag, strip off my t-shirt and painter's pants, and get ready for class. It is considered uncouth to wear undergarments with ballet clothes. I am completely naked behind the thin curtain. In ballet, bodies are just vessels for movement, not things that exist in their own right. I tug on my pink tights and yank a spaghetti-strap Danskin up to my waist. I stick my hand down the front of my tights and corral my pubic hair under the edge of my leotard. I pull another long-sleeve leotard, which has been butchered into a top, over my head and snake my arms through the straps of the Danskin.

I take my place behind Kim at the barre that's anchored to the wall below the grimy industrial windows. Kim is tall, with a long torso I envy. My short waist makes it impossible to do a fully horizontal seated forward fold, which means my hamstrings are perpetually cranky. On the other hand, I have almost perfect turnout. My legs rotate in my hip sockets a full ninety degrees, a feature only admired in ballet circles since it is rarely required otherwise. "Okay, ladies," Joffrey says. "Places please."

"It's Joffrey not Jeffrey," he had emphasized when I started taking classes with him. "Don't ever call me Jeffrey." Joffrey is Asian and completely hairless, near as I can tell. He clearly has no problem with errant pubic hairs, as evidenced by the skin-tight short shorts he wears as both his dancewear and streetwear. His white tank top is also painted on, and its plunging neckline shows off four gold chains, one of which is hung with a Chinese character made of jade.

We run through our barre drills. Pliés, battements tendus, battement glissés, ronds de jambes, fondus, frappés, petits battements, developpés, ronds de jambes en l'air, grands battements. High school French helps a lot here. In an hour and a half, it's reverence and we're done. I try not to slip on the slimy sheen that coats the floor on my way back to the changeroom. Perspiration is probably better than floor wax. Cheaper too.

"I don't know about you," Kim says, as she scrapes her tights off her sweaty legs, "but I always fart when I'm doing the jumps. Good thing the studio stinks so bad nobody would notice."

"Plus, it probably gives you a bit more lift," says Joanne. "I'll have to try it next time."

Joffrey stows his ballet shoes in a leather satchel, dons a set of sequined leg warmers and a pair of silver sandals, and heads off toward the stairs. "See you next week, ladies," he says. "Keep warm." Dancers are obsessed with staying warm. It's April but it's eighty degrees outside.

* * *

Don is looking at me like I told him his parking lot configuration sucks. I'm sitting in his office after giving him an update on the status of my systems librarian activities. The same status I gave him last month and the month before that and the month before that. The only person who ever comes into the library room is Bill, and the only book he ever uses is the *PDP 10 Machine Code Manual*. All the other well-classified books never leave the shelf, which means I don't need to spend any time returning them to the shelf. Nor do I spend any time classifying new books. We never get any new books. Which means I never have to regenerate my KWIC index. About once a week, I spend half an hour loading new software. I am so bored I'm tempted to start reading the *PDP 10 Machine Code Manual* to see what Bill finds so fascinating.

Everything is flowing along like a gentle stream. A gentle stream that's lulling me to sleep. No whitewater nor waterfall in the offing. Which is exactly why I've just told him I want to quit.

"You want to quit? Why would you want to do that?" he says. I tell him I want to take some time off. To do more dancing. I don't tell him I'm bored and I'm not sure I want to be a librarian and besides there's nothing for me to do here anymore. My work here is done. "I don't know what I'd do without you," Don says. "The operators won't know what to do without you either." That's pretty much true, Don. The only thing they'll have to talk about is the barely clothed Sunshine Girl du jour on page three of *The Sun*. I don't think any of them reads past page three, if they can even read.

"Okay," says Don. "Why don't you take a leave of absence, say six months?"

In this moment, I can't find a way to refuse this offer, so I un-quit. "Okay," I say. "See you in six months."

* * *

I get off the streetcar at Queen and McCaul and walk half a block north to Malabar. It's in an old warehouse building stuffed to the rodent-poop-rafters full of costumes, costume-making bits and bobs, and the complete gamut of ballet-dancing accoutrements. I'll need a new pair of pointe shoes if I start going to class every day.

The clerk climbs a rolling ladder and hands me down a box of Gambas, size three and a half. My feet are not size three and a half. They are size eight. The world of ballet requires shoving an ugly stepsister's foot into Cinderella's slipper. A pointe shoe is equally as fragile as glass; it lasts for roughly twelve hours of use. And in those twelve hours, there's a ten-minute window when wearing the shoe feels like kissing Prince Charming. Then the golden coach devolves into pumpkin pulp and the shoe is useless. I fork out forty-five bucks for the Gambas, buy a length of ribbon, and head back home. There's work to be done.

I sit cross-legged on the floor because I haven't made my bed back into a couch yet today. And maybe not tomorrow either. My baby-pink satin shoes rest in front of me, calmly awaiting surgery. I open my sewing kit and lay out my implements: scissors, needle, thread, moleskin, elastic, pen. After only a few hundred times, I succeed at threading a thin needle with even thinner baby-pink thread and proceed to stab my thumb into numbness as I attach a circle of elastic, just shy of the circumference of my ankle, to the heel of the Gambas. With my sewing shears, I sever four eighteen-inch lengths of inch-wide pink ribbon that's exactly the same shade as the shoes. These will be fastened precisely two and one-eighth inches from the heel, on a forty-five-degree angle. Ballet involves more math than I signed up for.

    I make intricate stiches with my tiny needle to ensure the integrity of the bond between the shoe and the ribbon. My minuscule needle continues to make not-so-tiny pricks in my thumb as I pull it through canvas on the inside of the shoe. A mere three hours later, I'm ready to fold over the top ends of the ribbons to bind them with still more microscopic stiches so they won't fray, and move on to the third-last step of the pointe shoe transformation process. I apply an oval of moleskin to the flat bit at the business end of the shoe to prevent the pretty pink satin from causing me to break a leg, which is probably why, in the dance world, you say *"merde"* for good luck instead of "break a leg." I turn the shoes over and mark one sole with an *L* and the other with an *R*. That's because pointe shoes out of the box don't care which foot they're on. They eventually develop a preference once your feet insist, but remain as indistinguishable as a set of identical twins.

    I painfully unwind my legs, get up from the floor, carry my Gambas into the bathroom and whack each leather instep a dozen times on the vinyl countertop. The guy upstairs stomps on the floor. "I'm going to tell Mr. Behrens you made noise after midnight," he yells. I personally think yelling at someone to shut up after midnight also counts as making noise. But no matter. The shoes are ready. I hold them up under the bathroom vanity light to admire my handiwork. There are smudges of blood on the bottom of the ribbons where it oozed out of my thumbs. This is kind of like putting the first scratch on a new car. There'll be more where that came from.

* * *

Kim stops to chat with me on the sidewalk after Joffrey's Friday morning class. "Hey, there's a new cowboy bar right across from Malabar. It's called Cowboys," she says. "Pretty original name. Let's go tonight. They have a mechanical bull and everything." I've seen *Urban Cowboy* four times. More for John Travolta than for the mechanical bull, but the bull at the new bar is probably a big draw for guys. I tell her to meet me at my place at eight.

I hear the doorbell ring just as I'm rummaging under the bed for my shoes. I open the front window, throw down my keys, and tell Kim to come on up. "I have some bennies," she says when she comes through the door. "They'll help us stay up late. I use them all the time so I don't feel hungry." I take the two red pills she offers me, in ballerina solidarity. We walk down to the St. George subway, go south to St. Patrick, walk west to McCaul, and down a block to the inner-city mall called Village by the Grange. Cowboys is decked out in barnboard siding and strings of patio lights. Kim and I crunch over the peanut shells on the floor as we claim two stools at a high-top table near the bar. We're both wearing black ballet slippers, old ones we don't use for dancing anymore, and Calvin Klein jeans over skimpy leotards. That's so guys will know we're dancers. "I'm sure if we sit here a little longer, someone will buy us drinks," Kim says. I have no legal tender except the subway token that's going to get me home, so I'm hoping she's right. Funny thing about not working. My bank balance is not going in the right direction.

Two guys sidle up to our table and ask if our empty chairs are taken. Bars are not allowed to serve you unless you are sitting down. Standing up with a drink might lead to dancing. Seating is at a premium, so I'm pretty sure they are angling for delivery of a beer rather than trying to pick us up. Especially since they look like Mormon missionaries, if Mormon missionaries wore Western shirts and bolo ties. They introduce themselves as Gary and Mark. They are almost indistinguishable. Short dark hair, clean shaven, square wire-rim glasses. "Are you girls dancers?" the Mark guy asks. Kim says yes and kicks me under the table. *See?* she mouths. I'm hoping they're thinking ballet not strip joint.

"Wow," says the Gary guy. "We're students at the chiropractic college. We'd love to come and watch you dance to study the body movements." I'm still not sure whether or not he thinks we're strippers, although my leotard leaves no doubt I don't have the boobs for it. The bartender brings us a bunch of drinks. DayGlo-green margaritas in fishbowls and Dos XX beers with no glasses. This seems to be what cowboys drink, since these same drinks are on every table. "Where do you dance?" says Gary. Kim explains about Queen Street and Joffrey and our daily class and our rehearsal for *Swan Lake*. Thank goodness. At least now the potential stripper notion has been laid to rest. The guys look a little disappointed. But not too disappointed to buy us another round.

I notice there's a crowd gathered around the mechanical bull. It's exactly like the one in *Urban Cowboy*, set on a platform like one of those coin-operated kiddie horses at the grocery store, but with no front or back end. The onlookers whoop and holler, just like cowboys should, as the bull challengers take their turn for a triumph or a tumble. "We came here for the bull," Mark says. I'm impressed they're willing to try since, so far, the bull has demonstrated complete mastery of how to buck-off riders within ten seconds. "Not to ride it," Mark continues. "We're here to hand out cards for the chiro school clinic. That thing is a sure path to a herniated disk. We get a commission for every referral."

By last call, the margaritas have not made a dent on my buzz from the bennies. My brain feels like a combination of a pinball machine on tilt and a strobe light. I can't tell if my vision is blurry or if they've turned on a fog machine. Kim looks calm and collected. I guess I'm not cut out for uppers. I rev too high at the best of times. I can't even tolerate caffeine. "You girls want to share a cab with us?" says Gary. Or maybe it's Mark.

"Sure," says Kim. "Drop me first." Kim lives way up at Keele and Lawrence. This does not seem to be a very efficient route since my place is on the way. Then I realize she's making sure she won't get stuck with the cab fare. I need to pay more attention to her money management tactics. When we get to her place, Gary, or maybe it's Mark, gets out too. Kim winks at me and says, "See you in class Monday."

"1740 Avenue Road," Mark, or maybe it's Gary, says to the driver. I'm pretty sure this was decided long before we got in the cab. I'm guessing Kim had something to do with it. It's what bohemian dancers would do. It's the opposite of librarian good sense. But isn't that what I've decided? Not be a librarian? On the plus side, at least I didn't have to spend my subway token.

I wake up when the sun hits the open venetian blinds. For a few minutes I have no idea where I am, then I remember mechanical bulls and margaritas. I hear water running in a bathroom, then the sound of a coffee machine. I pretend I'm still asleep. Gary, or maybe it's Mark, comes in and sits on the bed. "Hey, you," he says, "I have to go to that mandatory herbalist class. I'll be back by noon, though, then we can get some brunch." I mumble and feign sleep until I hear the outside door close and lock. This is my cue to launch out of bed with the singular purpose of getting the heck out of here. I forage for my clothes and find my leotard and jeans, but no underwear. I silently curse Kim and her quasi-legal drugs. I do not think I'm a very good free-range artistic type, although Mark, who might actually be Gary, may not agree. Fortunately, I don't remember giving Mark or Gary my phone number. Or real name. If I don't remember, it must have never happened.

Thankfully, I board an empty elevator on the trip down to the street. I slink through the lobby, with my head down in case there are security cameras. Once I'm outside, I find the nearest transit stop and relinquish my hoarded token to the southbound Avenue Road bus. I snooze through the bulk of the journey, then get off at Tranby, just north of Bloor, and walk a block west to Bedford Road. By habit, I glance up at The Cat's window just before I get to the porch. I am almost sure I see the curtain falling back into place. Does he just sit there all day? Maybe he'll think I was out at an early ballet class. Deranged hair. Sweaty leotard. Smelly armpits. Sounds about right. Even to a lawyer.

6

Prairie Girl

<u>1981</u>

After a hundred and twenty classes, fourteen pairs of toe shoes, and two burgeoning bunions, I am no closer to being anywhere near the level where someone would pay me to dance unless it involved poles and six-inch heels. The only thing I'm closer to being is broke. Time to do something about that. My bare feet pad down to the lobby to collect my Saturday morning newspaper, the place where all the hot job postings show up. I have no intention of going back to Dataline. I need a new life. Despite the glamour of grungy ballet studios and DEC 10 computers and dating lawyers, I feel like the time I waited in an endless line outside Maple Leaf Gardens to buy a Rod Stewart ticket. Nothing is moving an inch. I just wish I knew what direction I wanted things to go.

 I pick up the Saturday *Toronto Star* off my coffee table and page through it to the business section. There are job ads in various sizes, from one-inch three-liners to full-pagers. The size of the ad likely correlates directly to the level of desperation. A half-page item, under the banner of the Saskatchewan Research Council, catches my eye. "Manager,

Business Information Centre," it says, and goes on to describe the job, the fabulous city of Saskatoon, and the allure of the wide-open spaces of the prairies. Maybe a change in venue would be good. Maybe I do want to work in an actual library after all. Maybe my social life will improve. The charms of being a bohemian have turned out to be less than charming. Kraft Dinner. An unpaid tab at Malabar. Prospects that fizzle before the first date.

I'm still out at the ballet studio every day and don't want to miss a call for an interview. I need an answering machine. Answering machines are going for a hundred and fifty bucks, or half of what my apartment costs each month. Only lawyers and chiropractors can afford them. But I can rent one. I take the bus up to the answering machine rental joint at Avenue Road and Lawrence, fork out a fifty-dollar deposit and a promise to pay ten dollars a month, and come back with my prize. The first thing I need to do is record an outgoing message on the cassette tape. I guess it should have background music. I drop *The Greatest Hits of the 1700s* onto the turntable, place the needle down at the beginning of "Pachelbel's Canon," and in a soothing voice, ask callers to leave a message after the tone and to have a nice day. Because that seems like something you ought to say.

Karen thinks my answering machine is hilariously bourgeois. "Whoever calls you is going to think you're rich," she says. "Like The Cat." Karen proceeds to call me when she knows I'm out and leaves me prank messages. When I get home, I know not to get too excited about the flashing red light. Chances are it's just Karen, saying something like "I didn't hear the beep. Can you hear me?" or "I'm sorry, I must have the wrong number. Is this the right number? I've got your number, baby." Or occasionally it's The Cat, who begins all of his messages with a pause that lasts almost the length of the tape, like he's forgotten why he called, before saying, "I'm too busy cramming for the bar exam to get together. I'll talk to you some time." Otherwise, he only phones me after midnight when he's half drunk, waking me up to lament the fact that we didn't go out that night. I put the phone receiver by my pillow so I can avoid falling too far out of sleep and listen to The Cat breathe softly between his random sentences. "You're so sexy. My car's in the shop. Landlords are not allowed to kick you out of your apartment without ninety days' notice." I routinely wake up in the morning to the *beep-beep-beep* of a phone that's off the hook.

The red light is flashing when I get back from dance class. I am giving the red flashing light quite a workout. I hope it doesn't pack it in before I return the answering machine. I ignore it while I rinse out my sweaty leotard in the sink, hang it on the shower curtain rod, and forage in the fridge for something to eat, trying to remember how long the leftover Chinese food has been hanging around. I turn on the television to watch the news on Citytv, wash my dishes, alphabetize my records, and put new ribbons on my pointe shoes. Just before bed, I check my messages to see whether Karen has come up with anything new to say. Sure enough, Karen, in a very bad Greek accent, says she is calling from the Deep River Restaurant. "You order pizza? Fifteen minute, be ready," she says, before choking down a snorting laugh. But then, there's a real message. From the Saskatchewan Research Council. They want to do a phone interview tomorrow at two.

* * *

Bersani & Carnevale is a long thin restaurant on the northern fringe of Yorkville. It has a bar on one wall and banquettes on the other. Tiny tables line the front window, usually occupied by snappily dressed Italian guys drinking espresso and closing some deal, which may or may not involve offers that can't be refused. It's the kind of Italian place that does not sell spaghetti and meatballs or pizza. The kind of Italian place that makes Toronto's 1980s head spin. They refuse to put parmesan cheese on any pasta that involves shellfish.

The lunchtime seats at B&C are regularly filled with Dataline bums because it's around the corner from the office, and that is the case today. Fenella's getting married to Jim, one of the programmers, so Don's taking her out to lunch to celebrate, and she's invited me. I enter the restaurant wearing my typical ballet streetwear: enough layers of ripped and doctored retired dance clothing to create a reasonably complete ensemble, intending to project equal parts punk and enigmatic. My ears are embellished with a dangling purple plastic triangle on the left, and a gold-toned Mickey Mouse hat on the right, accompanied by a silver skull in the piercing further up my ear. I slide my punkish backside into the vacant chair beside Fenella. She looks me up and down and says, "You look like the furball my cat barfed up this morning, Carr. Good thing you have a new job, you'll finally be able to buy some decent clothes. If they even sell decent clothes in Saskatoon."

Don looks baffled. "New job? What new job? You have a job. Right here. Whenever you decide to come back."

"Oops," says Fenella. "I thought you would have told him by now."

Thanks a bunch, Shaw.

***

1981

The queue for the taxis at the Saskatoon airport consists of me. Good thing I don't have to wait, because the unfriendly wind out from the west has forgotten it's only September. The back seat of the cab is a forensic record of the past hundred passengers, who were big fans of McDonald's, chain smokers, and the type of people who apply the dregs of mascara in the back seat of a cab, enroute to some place for which mascara is a must.

I've only ever been to Saskatchewan once before, when I was passing through it with Bob on our way to Calgary, along a straight line of highway that reflects Winnipeg through the rearview mirror for an entire day. The trip into what passes as downtown Saskatoon takes me through an expanse of flatness that would challenge a pencil to wobble, and past the imaginatively named Avenues A, B, and C, which are lined with ancient bungalows with barren front yards that have given up hope on grass or vegetation of any kind. Perhaps I shouldn't have signed up for this sight unseen.

The Saskatchewan Research Council lives on the western edge of the University of Saskatchewan campus in a squat brown building built sometime in the last century. I get out of the cab, carrying a cloud of cigarette aroma with me, and yank down the skirt of my grey suit. The slits on the side are now sewn shut, which solved the thigh-high problem but makes it ride up instead. I should buy a new suit, but I don't know what people wear around here, so I'm going to wait until I find out. I walk up crumbling steps covered in permanent salt stains. At least I hope they're permanent. It couldn't possibly have been necessary to de-ice them this early in the fall. There's a receptionist sitting behind a thick wooden desk that's perpendicular to a smaller stenographer's table, which holds an IBM Selectric. I'm somewhat relieved to see it's not a manual typewriter, although the receptionist looks like she's been typing since they were invented. She is wearing a matching sweater and cardigan in pastel pink, and two strands of pearls. I hope this is not a display of Saskatoon high fashion. I cannot see her feet, but I'm certain they are shod in lace-up Oxfords. She has an intercom on her desk that looks kind of like a cable TV converter, brown plastic with three rows of buttons. She presses the one on the lower left. "Mr. Sharp, this is Mildred here at the front desk. Your appointment is here," she says. She does this even before I open my mouth. I guess they don't get many visitors around these parts.

Mr. Sharp introduces himself as "Mr. Sharp." He looks exactly like he sounded on the phone: about fifty, balding, and clearly a fan of meat and potatoes. His grey argyle sweater vest covers a white shirt with the sleeves rolled up to the elbows. But he greets me with a smile and a warm handshake. "Let's start with the fifty-cent tour," he says. "Then I'll show you to your office." We walk down a corridor covered in bile-green asbestos tile, past a black-and-white gallery of photos showing various men in lab coats. "Those are all the scientists of the month," he says. As we pass several labs full of beakers and guys wandering around in hazmat suits, he tells me about the research stuff they do, like how to improve wheat crop yields and expanding the usages for potash. There is also something to do with molybdenum. I feel like I'm back home in Deep River, as equally mystified about what goes on here as what went on in the nuclear research plant where my dad worked.

My fiefdom is the business information centre, which is library-speak for a library that's housed within a company. It's a real library, though, with thousands of science books and monographs, three racks of journals with names like *Agriculture Today* and *Livestock Weekly*, and a reading area. I have an office with a window and a door. The door actually closes. I'm being paid twenty-five thousand dollars a year. Almost twice what Don was paying me. Exactly my age. Without the three zeros. "Make sure you make your age," Karen said. "That's the biz school motto. Otherwise, tell them you have other opportunities."

I'm expecting I won't even have to do much librarian-ing. I have a staff of five, all of whom are at least ten years older than me, including Margaret, who looks to be in her late fifties. Margaret is the senior library technician and also acts as my assistant. Her job is to schedule the staff, proofread the computer printout of the KWIC index, and enter new books into the card catalogue. Bryce looks after library loans and searches the library database services to answer research questions. Mary Pat manages the budget and orders new books. Stephanie is the junior clerk, who shelves and dusts the books, picks up my lunch from the cafeteria, and takes my laundry to the dry cleaner. Looks like my job pretty much boils down to unlocking the door in the morning and locking it at night. Maybe they hired me because you can only have an official library if there is an official librarian on staff.

Dr. Pepper is the CEO, but there is no Dr. Coke or Dr. Orange Crush. Dr. Pepper's specialty is holding inspirational all-hands meetings every second Friday, wearing a grubby lab coat he never takes off and sporting an Einstein hairdo. Same round wire-rim glasses too. "We strive to be outstanding in our field!" he says. "We are potash pioneers! We can row that boat ashore!" I have no idea what he's talking about, and maybe nobody else does either. It's hard to tell because they all watch him with rapt attention. I just show up for the crustless egg-salad sandwiches so I won't have to make dinner.

* * *

Phil and Owen are always first through the door to the reading room when I turn the key at eight thirty every morning. Phil heads straight for *Agriculture Weekly* like it's a *People* magazine with Kim Bassinger on the cover. Owen's more of a *Chemistry Chronicles* kind of guy, looking for the latest molybdenum news. Today's Tuesday, the day I sort through the mail Margaret leaves on my desk. I save up the mail so I can anticipate the excitement of the day I get to open the mail. The second most exciting day is the day I reserve for signing the subscription cheques that Mary Pat leaves for me. That's because it provides the chance to continue to perfect my manager signature. Should it be forehand or backhand? Dot on the *i* or not? I briefly experimented with an *i* circle, then lowercase everything, before moving on to different versions of illegible, to imply I'm so busy I don't even have time to write my own name. So far, nobody's ever noticed that one signature never looks like another. This is either a failure on my part or on their part.

The letter on the top of the correspondence says it's from the National Library. It must be important. Maybe it's my nomination to the Library Hall of Fame. I open it first. *Dear Sir or Madam*, it says. *We have just received our depository copy of* An Investigation of Potash Amelioration in Crop Rotated Soil *and imagine our surprise that it contains cataloguing in publication data, yet we cannot recall doing the cataloguing.*

I know what this is about. Two months ago, Dr. Asher from the chemistry lab made an appointment to see me at my office. Clearly, Dr. Asher rarely darkened the door of the library, since if he had, he would have been aware that the competition for my time hovered around the same level as the rivalry for a slice of the morning after's cold pizza. On the plus side, having a meeting on my calendar gave me something to look forward to. Margaret ushered Dr. Asher into my office at the appointed day and hour with great deference and offered to get him a coffee. Margaret made it very clear when I started that she was not a stenographer and did not fetch coffee. I guess Dr. Asher was an exception. He turned out to be very friendly and relaxed. His lab coat was so white it must have cornered the market for Oxydol, and the fringe of red hair that ringed his scalp just above the ears emphasized the blue of his left eye and the brown of the right. He reached for Margaret's proffered mug of coffee, asked me how I liked Saskatoon, and told me how much he admired librarians.

I mumbled something about how Saskatoon was such a unique place, then waited for him to tell me what the meeting was about. "I have a new monograph coming out soon," he said. "I would like you to look after the cataloguing in publication." He slid a thick file folder across the desk and told me he was particularly proud of this one. "This could revolutionize crop rotation methods," he said. "It needs to get a place on the shelf that will get it the most attention. I'm sure it could be my ticket to a Nobel prize." Finally. Something important to do. I told him I'd have it ready in a week.

The next day, I got Stephanie to pull two dozen books off the shelves in the potash section, which in our library, spans about fourteen shelf-racks, so I could examine their cataloguing information in detail. The key to a precise call number lies in the artistry after the decimal point. I took Dr. Asher's monograph home for the evening. This was the most excitement I'd had in Saskatoon so far. A pre-publication book! About potash! It took me another few days of careful consideration, but at last I had it. I would place Dr. Asher's book, in perpetuity, in Dewey Decimal 633.9231589920. I entered this on the National Library form he gave me and slipped it in an express mail envelop.

We have no quibble about the quality of the cataloguing, the letter went on to say, possibly the first usage of the word 'quibble' in a business correspondence. *However, we would appreciate it, in future, if you would go through proper channels.* Wait a minute. I guess Dr. Asher didn't mean for me personally to do the cataloguing. I guess the National Library was supposed to do that.

Margaret sticks her head through my doorway and asks me how mail day is going. "I noticed there was something from the National Library," she says. "I bet it's something exciting."

"Oh, just a form letter," I say. I stuff the letter in the waste basket, underneath a pile of used teabags. Am I really a real librarian if the National Library doesn't trust me to catalogue an obscure research monograph nobody's even going to read? Am I really a real librarian if all I do is sit in my office and talk to my hoya plant? Do I really want to be a real librarian? Right now, I don't think I have a choice. They moved me out here and all. I'll have to make the best of it.

* * *

Since I have my very own library, I get to make my very own library rules. Forget about the no eating thing. The reading room table has turned into a satellite lunch room. My staff and

I gather at noon, along with the library groupies, including Phil and Owen. I unwrap my tuna sandwich and poke the straw through my cranberry juice box. For efficiency, and because I have not much else to do on the weekend, I make all my sandwiches Sunday night, then freeze them. This works better with cheese than with tuna salad, I'm learning.

Today's topic of conversation is Agribition. Agribition is like the Calgary Stampede, but for wheat. Agribition is the most exciting thing that happens in Saskatchewan. "Just saw in the paper today they're moving Agribition a week forward because it conflicts with the Grey Cup," Owen says. I stand corrected. The Grey Cup is the most exciting thing in Saskatchewan. And both the most exciting thing and the second most exciting thing happen at the end of November. Outside. In a province pretty much guaranteed to have snow in September and in May. June is optional. Mary Pat says her parents will miss Agribition anyhow because they'll be on their way to Arizona by then, for the winter. "Harvest is in," she says. "The cows have a caretaker. Going to the farm this weekend though. Gotta help my mother finish the canning."

"The hogs were really good last year," says Margaret. "Pity to miss that."

"My aunt got first place in the butter tart contest for three years running. She put blueberries in them. Oh, I guess I wasn't supposed to give that away," says Bryce.

My neutral expression is betrayed by my involuntary eye roll. "What are you doing when we're closed for Agribition?" Stephanie asks. I tell them I'm going to Toronto. Maybe do some shopping. Go to the El Mocambo. Hang out on Queen Street West. The usual.

"And what would second prize be?" Phil says. "Two weeks in Toronto?"

7

Farm Boy

<u>1982</u>

My Saskatoon apartment is on Fifth Avenue. Karen laughed when I phoned to tell her this. "Is it near the Empire State Building, or more toward Central Park?" she said. "Hope you can make it there because, if you can't, I don't think you'll make it anywhere." It is the only high-rise in Saskatoon, so it is also the de facto skyline. Nobody lives downtown except me and the other renegades that are wild and crazy enough to reside in this apartment building. I'm on the eighth floor, which is really the twelfth floor, because there are four levels of above-ground parking underneath. Underground parking is not a thing in Saskatoon. Something about permafrost. I don't have a balcony, but I do have large windows that look north toward the South Saskatchewan River. I can see next week's weather working its way across the prairies, and I can watch the sidewalks as they roll up each night at six. There's more tumbleweed than people downtown after dark, but at least the tumbleweeds are out on the town. Unlike me.

The ad that lured me to my new job conveniently forgot to mention the iceberg-friendly winter weather and the summer that shows up for a week if you're lucky. Transit is a concept rather than an actuality in Saskatoon, so I walk to work every day, down Fifth Avenue, across the University Bridge over the river, through the campus to the SRC building. I have a transistor radio the size of my palm, which fits into my coat pocket. I crank it up to a top-forty station, so I can sing along to "Turning Japanese" and "China Girl" as I trudge through the snow. At this moment, popular culture has an Asian fetish.

It's morning twilight when I leave for work in January. The thermometer has not risen above zero degrees Fahrenheit since October, and there's ice fog hitting my face, which is what you get when it's too cold to snow and the water vapour crystalizes into particles that suspend in the air like a mist. A mist that is happy to use your cheeks as an arctic spa. I wear my mother's old muskrat coat that weighs about thirty pounds and smells like mothballs. The collar has rubbed down to the leather at the back of the neck, gaping to let the frigid air down my back. On the plus side, the late 1940s shoulder profile is right back in style. My nostrils are numb and the only reason I don't have snot running down my face is because it's frozen in my nose. One of the first things everyone was anxious to tell me was that Saskatoon is even too cold to harbour cockroaches, insects that can survive nuclear fallout. I'll give it that one, dubious, advantage over Toronto.

The weather and my SRC riches give me a good excuse to buy a new fur coat. I want a black mink, just like Liza Minelli wears in the Blackglama ads in *Vogue* magazine. She looks like she's on her way somewhere fabulous to meet someone more famous than she is. Somewhere she'll be keeping her coat on all night or taking it off immediately because she doesn't seem to have anything on underneath. I wonder what The Cat would think of that trick.

I tear out the page, put on my sad, shedding muskrat, and head out to furrier row, an entire block on the edge of downtown that's infested with fur stores. I eenie, meenie, miney, and mo my way to Folk's Finer Furs. I ring the buzzer at the front door to notify the people inside there's someone outside, and a white-haired man with a measuring tape around his neck ushers me in to the store. He looks at my ancient muskrat with disapproval. "You've come to the right place," he says. "You must be from out of town. That coat is no match for Saskatchewan."

I pull the crumpled Liza out of my pocket and show it to him. "I want one like this," I say. "Do you have one?"

"No," he says. This is a disappointment. I guess I need to try eenie, meenie, or miney. I stash Liza back in my coat and head toward the door. "Not so fast," he says. "I don't have one. But I can make you one. Just like in the picture." He tells me all he needs is a few measurements, and I'll have my coat in two weeks. He goes behind the counter to an adding machine. "I think we can do it with forty-two pelts. With tax, six-thousand even." I'm not sure what I thought it would cost, but it was definitely not six-thousand dollars. My credit card limit is only a thousand. The furrier has clearly seen the look on my face before. "We offer interest-free financing, as long as you pay within twelve months. How about five hundred down, and five hundred a month?" This I can do. I must do. I live on Fifth Avenue, after all.

* * *

I'm in the process of locking up the library when I think I hear my phone ringing. I don't know why we bother locking it. There's nothing to steal except books about potash. I turn the key the other way and walk back to my office. It is indeed my phone. I press the lighted button for the incoming line and pick up the receiver. Silence. I guess I didn't get to it in time. Then The Cat says, "When are you coming to town? I need you to come to town."

"How did you get this number?"

"I have my ways," he says. "And maybe I can have my way with you. Stay at my place."

I don't know how, but I'm pretty sure he already knows I'm coming to town for vacation. No point in denying it. "I'll be there on Saturday," I say. "Staying at Karen's."

"Why are you playing hard to get? You're always running away from me. Call me the minute you get in. We'll go out on the town. Tell Karen not to expect to see you until Monday."

I hang up and rethink my packing list. I'm wearing the coat, of course. And the pink cowboy boots. But I'm going to need some clubbing clothes and some fancy underwear that will likely not stay on for long.

My flight arrives at four and I cab it to Karen's place at Wellesley and Sherbourne. I still have a copy of her key, so I let myself in and take the elevator to the nineth floor. She has left a note on the counter. She's out doing laundry but will be back soon. "Order a pizza. I've rented *Urban Cowboy*." She'll probably be disappointed I'm going out. Maybe we can save the movie until Monday.

The Cat's phone rings and rings and rings. Just before it goes to the machine, someone answers breathlessly. "Hello," says Scott, The Cat's roommate. I ask him if Morris is there. "No," he says. "He's gone to some film festival in Montreal for the weekend. Can I take a message?" *Yes, I'll leave him a message*, my inside voice says. *Piss off, loser.*

"Just tell him I called," I say, and hang up. I do not leave him Karen's number.

A few minutes later, Karen drags her laundry bag through the door. "The mink! The mink! I want to see the mink!" she says. I do not mention The Cat. Or dancing. Or a dirty weekend that was supposed to last until Monday. "You look just like Liza Minelli in that *Vogue* ad, except you have too many clothes on." She talks about plans for the weekend like Sunday brunch, a matinée movie, and dinner at the Bloor Street Diner. "But I have to work during the week. The banque just started a new fiscal year, and they have firmly embraced the six-and-five-percent inflation-busting raise limits so I need to show up and look grateful. For sure you'll be having more fun that me." Karen works at a "banque" not a bank. The Banque National du Paris. Closest thing she'll get to Paris on her salary, she always says.

A week to myself to kick around the city sounds fine. It will blow the straw out of my brain and remind me what sushi is. And remind me that The Cat will never change his spots.

* * *

Thursday features typical Toronto-in-March sleet, so I decide to stay in and engross myself in Karen's collection of trashy magazines. The phone rings around five. I hesitate to pick it up, but then I decide it might be Karen telling me she's working late or wants me to meet her somewhere for dinner. But no, it's The Cat. "I've decided to knock-off early," he says. "It's Bay Street night out. Meet me at The Hideaway in Yorkville at seven. It's New Wave night and two-for-one happy hour. We can catch the early set." Then he hangs up.

How the hell did he get this number? I only have an hour and a half to get ready. Better start right now.

I dash from the Cumberland subway exit to the door of The Hideaway, a half flight down from the street. My mink is definitely not waterproof. I look like Liza Minelli has fallen into the swimming pool at the Ritz. Not exactly the entrance I had in mind. It's fully dark outside and just as dim inside the club. I pass the coat check girl, who has a ticket ready to give me, but I decline. I am not going to entrust my six-thousand-dollar investment to someone who has probably not graduated from high school. I scan the room and my eyes land on The Cat, who is standing near the bar with a bunch of guys. He sees me and waves. I pick my way through the cocktail tables.

He looks me up and down. "You got anything on underneath that?" he says. The guys snicker. The Cat reads *Vogue*? Maybe for the articles. "These are some colleagues from work. They missed the train home. Might as well cool their heels for a few hours. Get away from the wives." Right. So they'll be here for the duration. He doesn't introduce me but does pour me a glass from a pitcher of beer. I hate beer. I sip at it as I listen to them talk about deals and torts and year-end bonuses. Nobody says anything to me. I am clearly a poor substitute for Liza. I'm sure it must be nine o'clock by now. I check the clock on the wall over the bottles of scotch. McCallen, it says. It also says seven forty-five. I set my still-full glass down and pretend I'm looking for the bathroom. Instead, I wind through the crowd that's started to assemble. They provide my cover as I slip out the front door. It's still drizzling. I'll have to take my coat to Mr. Folk when I get back. He'll know what to do. He'd better. It's only half paid for. And I needed new boots anyway. You've used up all of your nine lives, Cat. There will be no tenth.

* * *

Phil is still sitting at the reading table on Friday night when everybody has already left. I'm ready to lock up. I put on my coat and jangle my keys to get his attention. He stands up but doesn't make a move toward the door. "You doing anything tonight?" he says. I stop and think. I don't need to think about whether or not I'm doing anything. It's a given I'm doing nothing. The question is, do I want to do something with Phil. Phil's a pretty cute guy, with dark wavy hair down to his collar. His favourite outfit is a madras shirt and Wrangler jeans. His work boots are always impeccably clean. There's one problem. I'm pretty sure Phil is married. On the other hand, this would be my first date in Saskatoon since I got here. My flimsy standards say, "Strangely, I happen to be free. Pick me up at my place at eight."

I lie flat on my bed to inch my skin-tight turquoise Jordache jeans up my legs, breathing in to get the zipper to zip. I really hope I don't need to go to the bathroom tonight. After I wrestle my feet into my pink cowboy boots, I open the paper to the entertainment section, which, in the *Saskatoon Star Phoenix*, is one page. Some live music would be good. If this date is boring, there'll be an excuse not to talk. I spot an ad for the Western Roadhouse. Debbie Bechamp and Peter Komisar are playing. Right here. In Saskatoon. Tonight. Peter was in all the bands in my high school years and Debbie's a country star from the Ottawa Valley. I was even at their wedding, where Debbie got up on the stage at the legion hall, slung her guitar over her wedding dress, and belted out "D-I-V-O-R-C-E." Maybe not the best choice of song at a wedding reception. Nonetheless, it was the highlight of the evening. Phil will be impressed that I know the band.

I meet Phil downstairs just outside the front door when he pulls up in a cab. He tells me his car is in the shop. "Let's go to the Western Roadhouse," I say. "There's a good band playing, from Ontario."

Phil looks dubious. "From Ontario?" he says. "At a Western bar? Oh well, we can always go somewhere else if it's a bummer." Bummer? Have we suddenly time travelled back to the 1960s? Phil also points out that the Western Roadhouse is in a kind of dodgy part of town.

"How dodgy could it possibly be?" I say. "It's Saskatoon, not Toronto. I could show you dodgy. Do you know there's an abattoir district in Toronto?" Phil has no reply for this, but tells the driver to take us to 33rd Street North.

The Western Roadhouse looks like a typical Old West saloon, but without the saloon doors. Saloon doors and Saskatoon weather do not go together. The major décor feature is wood. Wood floors, wood ceiling, and wood walls, uninterrupted by windows. Wood is kind of a status symbol in a place without many trees, if you can reconcile the notion of status with a dive bar. Phil and I grab a high-top table. Looks like the beverage options are beer or beer. Phil goes to the bar and comes back with a Molson Export in each hand. No glasses. I raise my civilized Toronto eyebrows as I wipe the table with the arm of my puffy-sleeve pirate blouse. Phil catches on. "I asked about glasses," he says, "and the bartender said they don't have any. Something to do with minimizing weapons during the fights."

The band takes the stage. It's Debbie and Peter, all right, decked out in their best Western wear: a calico granny dress and cowboy hat for Debbie, and an embroidered denim shirt for Peter. They launch into their first set. "Pretty groovy for Ontario," Phil says, as we get up to dance. Groovy? I wave at

Peter, who looks perplexed, then surprised. I'm ridiculously happy to see a familiar face, even if it's from my backwater home town. My happiness spills over to my impression of Phil. This date is actually going pretty good. The band finishes their set. Peter says something to Debbie and points over to our table.

We chat with them during the break. I talk about how I ended up in Saskatoon, leaving out the part about how much I hate it. Peter says their tour will take them right across the country, to all the hotspots for country music. After Saskatoon, it's Moose Jaw, then Grande Prairie and Prince George. Debbie tells us about her new single, "Take My Hand." "I'm going to sing it in the last set," she says. "I brought a bunch of records to sell," she says, "but I'll give you one for free, since you're from the Valley and everything."

Phil looks impressed. "I'm not sure we can stay until the last set," he says. "I told the sitter I'd be back by midnight." Sitter? I want to know more about this but I can't ask in front of Peter and Debbie. They head back on stage and the music starts up again. Too loud to talk. Phil points at his watch and starts to put on his jean jacket. It's eleven thirty. I retrieve my sweater from the bar stool and follow him to the door. We walk out of the parking lot to the road, in search of a taxi. "Cabs probably don't cruise out here this late at night," Phil says. "I think we'll have to hitchhike." Exactly the way I'd prefer to be driven home from a date.

We stand under the neon sign by the road at the entrance to the bar, where he sticks out his thumb. Miraculously, after about ten minutes, a dinged, salt-stained, rust-coloured pickup truck pulls over. I don't think its original colour was rust. "Good thing I'm with a girl," Phil says. "I'd be here until morning, otherwise." I avoid thinking too much about why a girl might be an asset to being picked up by an unknown guy who smells like he's just mucked out a cow stall. Phil opens the passenger door, slides into the seat, then leans out to reach his arm around my waist to pull me up on his lap, the only option for a place to sit. I kind of feel like I'm Debra Winger in *Urban Cowboy*, being swept away from Gilley's by John Travolta. I hope this night ends as well as the movie. But without the jealousy, affairs, people dying from lightning, and fist fights. Phil asks our free chauffeur if he can take us downtown to Fifth Avenue. "I can call the sitter from your place," he says. "Maybe she'll stay later. Maybe even overnight." My dry, cold, wind-swept prairie bedroom might be starting to warm up.

8

If I Can Make It There

<u>1983</u>

I don't know why I bought a day planner for 1983 because the only entries are the ones it came with. Although I am very thankful to know when I should be observing national doughnut day, the great swaths of unfilled appointment slots advertise the wasteland of my social life. Phil is officially unseparated. The Cat remains AWOL. Bob is a suburban dad. I need to give my idle hands a purpose.

Bryce boots up the terminal on his desk. He puts the phone receiver upside-down into an acoustic coupler that tethers us to the outside world and dials up one of the commercial online database services we subscribe to. I can hear the clicking and outer-space sounds from my office as the modem connects. Three hundred bits per second, which means it can send or receive about three hundred words per minute. Only someone unfamiliar with the average length of a scientific research paper would be impressed with this speed. Bryce types a command beside the blinking cursor and watches as the green lines of letters fill up the terminal screen. He pushes his gold wire-frame glasses up the bridge of his nose, adding another layer to the fossilized smudges already in place, and hunkers down for half an hour until the full text of *Bovine Ungulate Peripheral Magnetoreception: A Longitudinal Study* squeezes through the phone line and lands on the dot-matrix printer that sits on a repurposed book cart near his desk.

I'm immersed in my busy day, browsing this month's *Library Journal*, flipping through the book reviews, job ads looking for perfect librarians, and articles about how to be a perfect librarian, thinking about what I could be doing instead of wasting my life being a librarian. Somehow, I have traded a job as a snail-racing officiant for the glamorous life of a paint-drying supervisor. I must get myself out of here or I'll end up being married to a farmer, and a visit to the Army and Navy store to buy new rubber boots will be the highlight of my week. I close the magazine and toss it on my desk, where it lands face-down. On the back cover there's a full-page ad for the International Online Libraries Conference. April 12–14, New York, New York. Call for papers. I probably know more about computers than any other librarian, ever. Why not submit an abstract? What's the worst that could happen?

This gets me thinking about databases. We pay a lot of money for our database subscriptions. I know a bit about how databases work from Dataline. Surely we could invent our own. Or actually, surely I could invent our own. Automate the card catalogue, maybe. Beats sitting at my barren desk, staring out the window. This is a research joint. Might as well start researching. I grab my mink and head out the door. "Off to the science library," I say over my shoulder, in Margaret's general direction.

* * *

Margaret drops the mail in my inbox on a Monday morning. "Don't know what this fat one is. It's from somewhere called the International Online Libraries Conference," she says. I eye the letter, which feels like it's a ticking time bomb that I have no idea how to disarm. I could do what they do in the movies: throw the thick envelop out the window and run in the opposite direction, but that might cause a bit of a stir. And in general, excitement and libraries go together like peanut butter and caviar. Instead, I busy myself with watering the plant on top of my filing cabinet, straightening the pile of papers on my desk, and gnawing at my fingernails. What if they accepted my abstract? I decide I can wait until after lunch to open the mail.

On Friday at five o'clock, the Online Conference envelop still remains intact. I must bite the bullet before I go home because I certainly can no longer bite my fingernails. They are nonexistent. I lift the letter with the bloody nubs of my forefinger and thumb like it is a dirty diaper that's festered too long. I squeeze my eyes shut as I tear it open, as if that will shield me from the smell of the contents. I read the letter. "We are delighted to accept your abstract *Relational Databases: A Bold New World for Libraries.* We have scheduled you right after the keynote on the first day of the conference, in the main ballroom, because we think everyone will want to hear this presentation. Will forty-five minutes be enough? If not, call and let us know because we think this is a very important topic," it reads. It goes on to say my research paper is due at the end of March and that I will be responsible for bringing my own slides. Ballroom? Slides? Holy crap. One small thing I neglected to tell the Online Conference: aside from being in several high school plays, I have never spoken in front of an audience. Especially not an audience in a room that seats a thousand and is expecting me to wow them with a library innovation not seen since the rubber stamp.

* * *

Mr. Sharp adores eating lunch at the faculty club and I adore that he adores it because I get a free lunch once a month when we have our biweekly meeting. We are supposed to meet every two weeks but something important always comes up for Mr. Sharp and he cancels at the last minute. Except for being cheated out of a meal, this is okay with me. It's hard enough to find something scintillating to say about the library once a month. Except today. Today I have to get him to agree to foot the bill for my trip to New York.

We sit at his usual table, near the buffet. Once his coffee cup has been filled, I launch my first salvo. "You were talking about the importance of innovation last time. Remind me where we left off." Mr. Sharp leaps at my bait and chomps on it like a pelican fishing in the South Saskatchewan River. He proceeds to expound on how the SRC is positioning the prairies to lead Canada into the twenty-first century and become an economic powerhouse as a result of our innovation. "How important do you think information will be in achieving success?" I say. This sends him into a long monologue about how information breeds knowledge and knowledge is power. "And where do computers fit in?" I ask. Mr. Sharp pounds on the table with zeal.

"Computers are essential! We couldn't do it without them," he says.

"Then I have an idea," I say. "There's a thing called the International Online Conference. It's in New York this year.

If I deliver a paper I can attend for free. It will only cost travel. I can showcase SRC innovation by talking about applying technology to information."

Mr. Sharp pounds the table again. "Brilliant," he says. "See if you can make that happen." I nod and write in my notebook as if he's given me a great idea. I do not mention it's already a done deal.

* * *

The floors at La Guardia airport are the colour of dried mud. That's because they are covered in dried mud. At least two inches deep. Passengers' snack wrappers blow down the corridors like urban tumbleweeds past the security guards, whose rusty guns were probably bought on final clearance from the discount gun warehouse. They loiter in front of Dunkin' Donuts in the concourse, ignoring the Hari Krishna devotees accosting travellers for donations. I gear up to the purposeful clip of Toronto walking speed, which turns out to be about a tenth of New York City foot travel. I trail far behind the native New Yorkers as I head toward the ground transportation. Once I get there, the mass of people competing for a taxi is about as substantial as the huddled masses arriving at Ellis Island, except my rivals for a ride downtown are much less civilized. There is yelling and honking and finger gestures and no such thing as a line-up. If I can make it here, I can make it anywhere.

The cab drops me off at the Times Square Holiday Inn. This turns out to be less glamorous than it sounds. The lobby is crammed with a Japanese school group who, judging by the mountain of luggage, is planning to stay at least ten years. I try to elbow my way to the front desk, using my best Toronto subway skills. Once again, I'm no match for Manhattan's sense of self-preservation. Or maybe just no match for Tokyo subway skills. I squat down on my suitcase and practice my speech. Out loud. Nobody will notice over the two-hundred-decibel chatter surrounding me.

After I've run through my spiel a thousand times, I finally secure a key and head up to my room. The door opens on a walk-in closet. Oh, wait, this is the room. A single bed with a fold-down bedside table and hooks on the wall for clothes. There's not even a closet in this closet. I raise the window blind to reveal a view of the airshaft. No matter. I'm not here to hang out in a hotel room. I turn on the television as I unpack. "Breaking news," says a perky, well-coiffed woman. "Manhattan taxi driver finds woman's head in back seat. It had probably been there for two days, police say. Film at eleven." I do not think I will be tuning in at eleven. I do not want to think about where the woman's body might be, nor about a killer on the loose who likes to decapitate people. Nor about what's up with a taxi driver who fails to notice decomposing, renegade body parts in his place of work. Going out for a walk alone around Times Square may not be the best idea. I will go to bed instead.

The sound of a key in the lock wakes me with a start. I hear my hotel room door open, then snag on the safety chain. I leap out of bed, slam the door shut with my shoulder, relock it, then brace the door with my back. My heart has bypassed my throat entirely and is trying to get past my teeth out of my mouth. After ten minutes of barring the door with the heft of my hundred-pound body, there are no new sounds from the hallway. Perhaps the burglar-rapist-serial killer has moved on to more amenable victims. The advantage of a small room reveals itself at this moment. I can reach the phone. I press the quick-dial button for the front desk. It rings twenty times before someone answers. "What do you want?" says the desk clerk. I explain about my door. "What am I supposed to do?" he says. "If I had to do something every time a thug tries to break into a room I'd never be at my desk. Or get a proper lunch break."

My terror adrenalin repurposes itself into indignation adrenalin. I refuse to end up dead before I get to deliver the speech I've rehearsed for a month. I'd rather die of embarrassment on stage. "What you are supposed to do," I say, "is find me another room, send security up to escort me to the new room, and take the cost of the room off my bill." Mr. Sharp will be happy about that last part. The desk clerk is not equally as happy. My residual terror takes the conversation up a notch. "Did you not see on the news there was a woman's head being driven around in a cab for two days? What do you think would happen if my head ended up in this hotel room for two days? You can forget about any more Japanese tourists. And," I add as a triumphant final blow, "they will certainly fire the night desk clerk, who will never find another job because who would hire somebody that let a murder happen?" The clerk thinks about this for a minute, then tells me security is on their way up with my new room key.

I grab my clothes off the wall hooks, throw on a pair of jeans and a t-shirt, and shove the rest into my suitcase, just as the security guard knocks on my door. We head down to a second-floor room right beside the elevator. He unlocks the room. There isn't enough space for both of us at the same time, so I wait in the hall while he certifies the room is empty. Then he hands me the key. It's four in the morning. My presentation is at ten, right after the keynote. I doubt I'll sleep again. Maybe not ever. Certainly not in this hotel. Might as well practice my speech. Loudly. That's bound to keep any rapists and murderers away. It will knock them into unconsciousness immediately.

* * *

I arrive at the conference at seven o'clock. I have not had breakfast. Not because I want to save Mr. Sharp some money, but because I don't want to barf on my notes or anything else, like the crimson brocade ballroom broadloom that's coming in and out of focus under my feet as I try get my eyesight out of synch with my stomach. My red suit stands out like a cardinal in a hardwood forest in the sea of subdued black and grey librarian attire. Red suits are all the rage in Toronto, which makes me bleeding edge in Saskatchewan. But apparently, New York is not a place one chooses to stand out, unless you are Andy Warhol. My name tag has a green ribbon that says Speaker in gold letters, which hangs vertically from the pin that holds it on my lapel. I look like a reverse Christmas tree. The good news is that if it does become necessary for the floor to open up and swallow me whole, nobody will notice because I'm the exact same colour as the carpet.

The keynote speaker comes on and starts to talk, but I have no idea what he's saying. I'm too busy panicking and trying not to dwell on the fact that I really need to pee. Like, right now. The topic is the library of the twenty-first century, but I'll be lucky if I survive past lunch, let alone the year 2000. Just as I'm about to run to the bathroom, the master of ceremonies grabs me by the elbow. It's time to take my spot in the wings. Almost showtime. But without benefit of the pre-show spliffs we shared backstage in theatre arts. Or, more importantly, a bathroom break.

I take my place at the podium and start speaking. Suddenly, I see the MC frantically waving his hand at me, with five fingers splayed. The five-minute warning. Forty minutes have passed and I have absolutely no idea what I've said, but it must have been in some facsimile of English because the audience is nodding with approval. My memorized conclusion comes magically to my lips and I leave the stage with a nonshameful amount of applause. Mr. Fraser from theatre arts must have taught me some transferrable skills other than how to mimic exotic accents to pick up guys.

I join the herd heading to the coffee-break stations. Coffee is ill-advised, so I grab a granola bar and try to fade into the background. My red suit is having none of this nonsense. I'm *Where's Waldo?* in reverse, swarmed by delegates proffering their copy of the proceedings for my autograph, like we're at the librarian version of a Rolling Stones concert. Scratch that. Maybe more like a Lawrence Welk convention. Or like I have single-handedly invented the Venn diagram that intersects librarianship with rocket scientist.

* * *

When I get off the plane in Saskatoon, I feel like I've just exited from a six-lane highway on to a cow path. And not in a good way. On Monday morning, I get to work just after Margaret has unlocked the door. "How was New York?" she asks. "Was it like in the movies?"

"Sort of," I say. Like the kind of movie that involves severed heads and masked rapists. But also like a double feature, where the other movie involves Audrey Hepburn, sports cars, and cigarette holders. I tell Margaret I'll fill everyone in at the staff meeting after my semi-monthly lunch and head off to the faculty club.

    Mr. Sharp sets down his hot buffet plate on our usual table. "Nothing like prime rib day," he says. I'm going the cottage cheese and pineapple route, which is the only option other than beef, today and all other days. Not that I have anything against bovines. They make up half the population of Saskatchewan. I just never acquired a taste for their meat. "How did your little conference go? All those librarians! It must have been very quiet. I must say I was impressed at how low your expenses were." I do not mention the free hotel room, nor the reason for the free hotel room. Mr. Sharp digs into his meat, potatoes, and gravy and moves on to another, clearly more important, topic. The role of innovation and information in the twenty-first century has somehow been relegated to the back burner. "Did you hear Brian is experimenting with a new wheat blend that replaces insulation in telecommunications cable? And Dave thinks he has found a way to use potash as oven-cleaner." Clearly, there's no point in sharing my triumph with Mr. Sharp. He has moved on. Why do I work in a career that gets no respect? It doesn't even get the opposite of respect, which would at least mean it got some kind of attention. Librarians just get benignly ignored, like a baby in a playpen. On the walk back to the office, I decide what I'm going to do. It will take a bit of work and more than a few favours to call in, but if I can swing it, I'll be out of here before the snow flies. Which in Saskatchewan means September.

9

Business as Usual

1983

The University of Toronto faculty of management studies occupies a four-storey brown brick building at the corner of Bloor St. West and Bedford Road. The same Bedford Road that was the site of my first apartment and the same Bedford Road that ends in the block that holds Dataline's office. The business school's building also houses the faculty of social work, as if someone had tried their best to concoct the most diametrically opposed academic bedfellows and succeeded spectacularly. The nascent social workers are predominately women, with a few earnest men with high emotional IQs thrown into the mix. The budding business tycoons are predominately men, with a few hard-nosed women with exemplary quantitative skills thrown into the mix. In my incoming business school cohort of one hundred and twenty, there is a prison guard, an architect, a military officer, a nurse, a lawyer, an assortment of engineers, too many accountants, and me, a philosopher-librarian. I am one of twenty women. Except I happen to be missing both the hard nose and the quantitative skills. I have landed back in Toronto as a full-time MBA student. Class of 1985.

First-year classes are mostly conducted in the education building next door because there isn't enough room to accommodate us at home base. We all need to take the same core courses before branching out into subspecialties like Ponzi Scheme Fundamentals, Marketing Refrigerators in Antarctica, and Building a Better Mousetrap. We are split into two sections of sixty students. There will be the inevitable collateral damage along the way, both voluntary and involuntary. But I don't know that yet. I start out on my business school journey oblivious to potential perils lurking in the halls. And probably under the desks too.

My section shuffles into the classroom that will be our home for the next eight months, revisiting the middle school world where the subject teachers rotate but the students stay put. Ten o'clock is accounting. I find a seat near the middle, not close enough to the front to call attention to myself, and not too close to the back to be lumped in with the slackers and late-comers. The woman beside me looks like she already has business school beaten into submission. Not a single strand of her short dark hair moves out of place as she turns her head my way. The bow of her red silk blouse is tied in perfect symmetry at her collarbone. The toes of her sensibly heeled patent pumps peek discretely from under the hem of her black crepe trousers. Not pants. Trousers. She has pearl studs in her earlobes and a narrow chain belt around her waist. Her accounting text, ringed notebook, and gold Cross pen are laid out in a precise grid on her desk. I hate her fully and completely.

She nods at me and extends her impeccably manicured hand. "I'm Martine," she says. And then, lowering her voice,

"We women are going to need to stick together. I thought law school was overrun with men. This is ridiculous." The sea of Y chromosomes continues to flow through the door, swamping us in their prodigious wake. I introduce myself and tell her I just moved back from Saskatoon. "Hmmm," she says, as she regards my first-day-of-school outfit. Homemade camouflage shorts over footless ballet tights, topped with a hot pink bowling shirt I got at a thrift store on Queen St. West. It says my name is Fred. My legs disappear into my summer cowboy boots, the baby blue ones.

"I've never taken accounting before," I say.

"Me neither," says Martine. "And I'm terrible with numbers. Not much math required in law school." I think she's managed to slip in a reference to law school about two hundred times and she's only uttered three complete sentences.

Professor Bryant calls us to order and starts droning on about debits and credits. I take copious notes, hoping it will make sense when I read them again tonight. Karen told me not to expect any help from her. "I graduated over three years ago. I'd never get in now. It's much more competitive because of the recession. You are on your own, Carr."

When we break for lunch, I gather my books, stuff them in a canvas tote bag that bears the logo of a flour company, and walk quickly to the cafeteria. I want to fade into the background and crack open my finance text to see what exactly that is. Must be something to do with wheeling and dealing because all the guys are very excited about it. I must be prepared. I'm swimming upstream without benefit of water. Not a drop of it anywhere around these parts.

I take my toasted bagel with cream cheese to an alcove with orange vinyl cubes that are supposed to function as seating. I'm in the process of unwrapping my lunch when

Martine plops down on one of the cubes. She opens her leather satchel and pulls out a pristine waxed-paper package that holds sprouts, avocado, and roast turkey encased in whole wheat bread. "This is where you disappeared to," she says. So much for trying to hide. I eat my bagel, while she launches into her life story. Her parents sold their house in Oakville and moved to a huge condo near the campus so Martine and her sister could live there while going to U of T. "It's so embarrassing," she says. "Living with the 'rents when I'm already twenty-five." She talks about her articling job at a firm she calls Boring, Boring, DesLauriers & Binnington, and how bad she feels about ditching a law career after spending all that time and money. "You are so great to talk to," she says. I have not said a single word.

 We hit the bathroom before class, dumping our books on the sink counter. When we come out of the stalls, two older women, maybe teacher's college teachers, are waiting for the toilets. They eye our finance texts and one of them says, "Thank goodness women aren't stuck being teachers or nurses these days."

 Martine and I exit the swinging door that leads to the hall and burst out laughing. Who knows what we'll end up doing, especially if it requires passing finance first. I already looked. There are forty pages at the back of the book chock full of incomprehensible equations. Martine links my elbow with hers. "If we don't hang together, we'll all hang separately," she says. "I didn't get out of law school without learning that." Again with the law school. But now I've made a friend. I'll just have to convince her to come shopping at Courage My Love to fix her poor taste in clothing. "We're going to be good friends," she says. "I'll just have to take you shopping at Sportables to fix your poor taste in clothing."

* * *

I repatriated myself from Saskatoon with my fur coat and an overflowing bank account, courtesy of the lack of opportunity to spend my fat paycheque. I can afford a decent place to stay. Unfortunately, decent places are in short supply in Toronto. In the meantime, I'm floor surfing at Karen's bachelor apartment on a futon that gets stashed behind the couch during the day. When I get back from class on Wednesday, Karen tells me there's a message from The Cat. "I wrote it down somewhere," she says. "How did he get this number anyway?" I shrug and remind her he's a lawyer. He can probably track anybody down. Even if her last name is Smith and there are seven small-print pages of K. Smiths in the Toronto phone book. He's persistent, I'll give him that. Reliable, not so much. I have dressed up too many times only to be left ordering takeout pizza and watching *The Mary Tyler Moore Show* reruns, waiting for the phone to ring. "Darn. I can't find that piece of paper," she says. Just as well. He'll call back. Or he won't.

I finally find an apartment, on Sherbourne Street, just south of where Karen lives. I retrieve my meagre boxes from her basement storage space and drag them to my new place on a wagon. I have always strived to keep my stuff to a minimum. So far, I have not needed to move in the middle of the night, but best to be prepared. I've ordered a sofa bed that should be delivered tomorrow, and at least this time there's no contorted Victorian-era staircase to contend with. But first, as always, I've got to wait for the phone guy to show up. The phone-guy dispatcher always says to expect him between nine and four. In reality, there are only two times a phone guy ever arrives: nine or four. I have no idea what he does in between, but I have never met anyone for whom the phone guy showed up at ten or two or even three thirty. Also, the phone guy will only show up at nine if you are running late and don't get to your apartment until nine-fifteen. *Sorry I missed you*, the sign on your doorknob will say. *Please call to reschedule. Next available appointment: a week from next Tuesday.* Which is why I'm surprised that the phone guy arrives on my doorstep precisely as I pull my wagon up to 252 Sherbourne Street, at 8:47 a.m. This has got to be a good sign.

The phone guy volunteers to heft one of my boxes and trails behind me as I go to unlock my first-floor apartment. He gets busy unscrewing phone-box things and mysterious outlets, while I retrieve the remaining two boxes from the wagon. I start unpacking my kitchen stuff as he continues his installation tasks in the other room. I have a bachelor suite, but it has a separate kitchen and a nook near the bathroom that could be a dressing room. It's got a cove ceiling and leaded glass in the window, which overlooks a public parking lot. It was probably a fancy place to live at one time. Not this particular time. But it doesn't smell, it's right on transit, and it fits my student budget.

I finish in the kitchen and go back into the main room just as the phone guy is starting to pack up his tools. He looks kind of grim. I hope he got the phone working. "What do you do?" he asks. I'm not sure how this relates to the task at hand, but I tell him I'm a student. "Can you afford to move? Is this your only option? I'd get out of here right now if I were you." This is odd. Here I am finally fully prepared to move on a moment's notice and suddenly someone thinks that's exactly what I should do. "I have never seen so many cockroaches in my life," he says. "The entire wall cavity is teaming with them. I hope none got into my tool bag. I'm going to write up a report. This place is going to be blacklisted. You're lucky I finished the job." The phone guy backs out of the apartment, keeping an eye out for any cockroaches that might want to follow him home like eager puppies.

I pick up the phone and confirm there is, in fact, a dial tone. I call Karen and beg her to let me sleep on her futon one more night. I'm not bunking at my place until I can elevate myself above the bugs. I'm pretty sure cockroaches just stick to walls and floors. That would make sense, wouldn't it? I'll buy some diatomaceous earth. Everything will be just fine.

The next afternoon, my new phone rings for the first time. I pick it up and say, "What now, Smith?" Karen is the only person who has my number. There's silence on the other end. I'm about to hang up when a familiar voice starts to speak.

"Heard you were back in town," says The Cat. "Business school. Quite impressive. Come over to my place later. After seven. We'll go out somewhere." He hangs up. I couldn't have said anything anyway. It's hard to talk when your jaw is on the floor.

Instead of preparing a case for tomorrow's marketing class, I spend the rest of the day figuring out what to wear. I need to look casually disinterested yet irresistible. Cowboy boots for sure. My strappy leotard top. Sweatshirt with the neckline slashed so it falls off my shoulder. Calvin Kleins. I head to the corner of Sherbourne and Carlton to catch the westbound streetcar. As I wait, a car rolls by me slowly and the man driving it lowers the passenger window. "Going somewhere?" he says. "Want a lift?" I shake my head and look down the street to see if there's a streetcar rounding the corner from Parliament. Nothing. Another car slows down, and another man asks me if I need a ride. Then five minutes later another, and another. This is just weird. Nobody in Toronto is that nice.

I walk closer to the corner. Maybe there's a northbound Sherbourne bus that will take me to the subway. That's when

I notice something. All the way from Carlton to Gerrard, every ten feet or so, there's a woman standing at the curb. The one closest to me is wearing white thigh-high, wet-look platform boots, satin short shorts, and a halter top that barely contains her considerable assets. Right. Street commerce. The underground economy. I'm betting there are also a few dope dealers hanging out in the park. I should propose this topic for my economics essay. I'll have lots of research material. The streetcar finally shows up. The door wheezes open and I walk up the steps, drop my token in the box, and snag a seat that miraculously does not have gum on it.

I arrive at The Cat's building on Quebec Avenue near High Park just before seven. I check out my reflection in the mirrored tile on the wall of the lobby. A little sweaty from the subway ride, but otherwise in good order. I press the button beside The Cat's apartment number and wait for him to buzz me in. Nothing. I press the button again. Still nothing. I press it once more. This is ridiculous. I decide to wait five more minutes, max. I'll have to guess how long that is, though. I still do not own a watch. At about the four-minute mark, the door buzzes. "Come on up," The Cat says through the intercom.

He is standing in his doorway when I get off the elevator. "I'm just jumping in the shower," he says. He's got Naked Eyes on the stereo, singing "Always Something There to Remind Me." I sit down and flip through a *Lawyer's Quarterly* that's lying on the coffee table. I can hear him in the shower and it feels kind of weird so I go out on the balcony and lean against the railing, looking south to the lake, what little I can see beyond High Park.

The shower stops and a few minutes later The Cat comes up behind me, wraps his arms around my waist, and breathes into my ear. "Why did you need to run away to Saskatoon?" he says. I get the familiar flutter in my gut. He leads me back into the living room and goes into the kitchen to open some wine. We sit on the couch drinking Chardonnay. The Cat launches into a monologue about how stressful his job is and that he only gets the shit legal-aid cases and that his new roommate is a deadbeat. Meanwhile, he tries to stuff his foot down the top of my boot. "Looks like two could fit in here," he says. I have no idea what that's supposed to mean. The clock ticks on with no sign we're going anywhere or eating anything. "I guess it's time for bed," he says.

His alarm goes off at six the next morning. I get up too because I need to go home and change before I head to class. The Cat busies himself with getting dressed, making coffee, and pulling papers together for his briefcase. I grab my clothes from various places on the floor, find my boots, and open the front door. "See you around," The Cat says. "I'll be pretty tied up for the next while." I close the door. Not gently. At least the girls standing on Sherbourne St. get paid. I didn't even get dinner. That's it. I promise I will never speak to him again.

* * *

Much to my surprise, I like accounting. Accounting has many rules. Rules that are immutable. You either get it right or get it wrong, and there are all kinds of insidious ways to get it wrong. But when you get it right it's a thing of beauty. It is the polar opposite of philosophy, where there are no right answers. Just right questions.

Martine and I huddle together in Professor Bryant's class. It's winter, so I've swapped my camo shorts for army fatigues and am wearing my winter cowboy boots, the pink ones. My black mink coat is draped over the back of my chair. Karen calls it the "schmink." "You're always swanning around in that schmink like you're from New York or something," she says. My fellow students, on the other hand, look more askance at my inner-wear than outer-wear.

Professor Bryant is explaining prepaid rent. He tells us that some leases require a twelve-month payment up front. If this is paid in January, and it's for $12,000, you might be tempted to claim the entire expense in the same month. If you did, not only would you flunk accounting, you would probably end up in jail. This is another thing I like about accounting. It's so dangerous that it's easy to end up on the wrong side of the law. That's how they caught Al Capone, after all. Philosophers, on the other hand, rarely get in trouble with the police. Only with angry mobs carrying pitchforks.

In the accounting final exam, Professor Bryant trots out all the greatest hits. Depreciation, payroll remittances, subscription revenue, and entertainment expenses. My pencil gets worn down to a nub and my eraser is reduced to a grubby pink pea as I swap credits for debits and swap them back again. Just in case. Professor Bryant gives us the five-minute warning. I check my answers one last time. I am truly an accounting Michelangelo. I shrug on my mink and drop my exam booklets on Professor Bryant's desk.

Martine is right behind me. "Let's head over to the Pits and compare notes," she says. Martine does not have anything less than an *A* in her alphabet. Even the appearance of an *A-* induces severe trauma. I, on the other hand, stand by the medical school rule: even the person who graduates at the bottom of the class gets to call themselves a doctor. Not that I'm deliberately trying to slide through just under the wire. I just want to have a life outside of the classroom.

The Pits is the student lounge in the basement of the B-school building. It has no windows and smells like eraser dust and stale beer, punctuated with whiffs of student angst. We share it with the proto-social workers but manage to keep them mostly at bay with our swagger, bravado, and loud arguments about how to choose the right interest rate for discounted cashflow calculations. The mere mention of cashflow strikes fear into their bleeding-social-justice hearts.

Martine and I head toward the corner to a couch that started out orange but is now brownish. Martine fishes a cotton handkerchief out of her purse and places it on the cushion before she sits down. "What did you do with question twelve?" she asks. I have to think carefully to remember what question twelve was.

"Right. The landlord one," I say.

"Yes," says Martine. "The one with the prepaid rent. I wasn't sure if I needed to expire it over twelve months or eighteen months." Crap. I forgot to expire the prepaid rent! I practically have that tattooed on my forehead. I have probably failed miserably. And if I do, it will be because of the bell curve. Everything is graded on the curve. The theory of the curve is that everything follows a normal distribution. Hence, half of the students should fall above the median and half below, and only twenty percent should get an *A*. The person who decided bell curves were a good idea had apparently never been faced with a class full of MBA students. There is no such thing as below average. Average is not in our lexicon. But I'm proving I'm surprisingly good at logical things and business courses are surprisingly straight forward. So far.

10

Greed Is Good

<u>1984</u>

The Management Information Systems course is about computer applications that automate business functions and support decision making. Professor McCandless describes them to us passionately as he swaps acetates on the overhead projector. The timesaving! The insights! The paperless office! I could tell him a thing or two about the nonexistent paperless office. If computer companies like Dataline can't even figure out how to use less paper, there's no shred of hope for anyone. But as Tracy Kidder said in *The Soul of a New Machine*, "computers are the heart of businesses today" and I'm here to learn all about it.

Professor McCandless looks kind of like Bill Gates. Clean cut. Square wire-rim glasses, and a pocket protector holding an assortment of pens and mechanical pencils. If this was twenty years ago, he'd have a slide rule holster on his belt. Instead, he wears a digital watch the size of a coaster that beeps at random intervals. Ironically, this is one of the few classes that does not require the closest thing we have to a computer, the HP12C programmable financial calculator we had to buy when we started school, state of the art for the time. And $120. Worth two pairs of Calvin Klein jeans but nowhere near as sexy, in my opinion. The guys beg to differ. They spend every spare moment trying to teach the HP12C new tricks, like how to ace the finance exam.

I am the only person in my class who has ever told a computer what to do. I doodle as Professor McCandless talks about databases, terminals, and modems. Everyone else seems mystified. This is understandable since Professor McCandless has nothing to show us other than photocopied pictures of mainframes with guys in white shirts standing in front of them, their sleeves rolled up to the elbows and wearing ties with clips so they don't end up being strangled by the tape drives. The guys in these photos always look more puzzled than pensive, as they gaze toward the hardware. As if they aren't quite sure how they got there. Kind of like me and business school.

Professor McCandless tells us all about how businesses will use computers for competitive advantage. "Sounds like science fiction to me," Martine says. "How can anyone possibly do well in a subject where everything is invisible?" I tell her it's not actually invisible. There's input and output and reports that show you whether or not the computer's doing what you asked it to do. "Whatever you say," says Martine. "Doesn't make it any less baffling."

MIS is the least popular course, maybe because it's not entirely clear how you would make money at it. Most people want to be bankers or accountants or hedge fund magnates. I'm pretty sure I don't want to be any of those things. I like MIS. I like knowing things about how to make computers do stuff. I have a secret power that nobody else has. At the very least, I can crush the MIS bell curve.

***

Everybody is busy lining up summer jobs, especially those that might lead to a full-time job offer. Martine is going to National Grocers. Roger is going to General Motors. Glen is going to the Bank of Montreal. I do none of these things. I don't even attend the summer job recruitment fair. I am going back to Dataline. No interview or competition required. Through Fenella, I learned the librarian who replaced me is going on maternity leave at the end of April. Don is overjoyed I'm available to fill in. Not only do I have a summer job, I have a part-time job all the way through second year, for the princessly sum of ten dollars per hour.

I ride my bike north on Sherbourne, take a left to join Bloor, and veer right on Church, which curves around to join Davenport Road. I lock my bike outside the Dataline building, click off my pannier bag, and head to my first day of old work. No suits this time around. I stick with my casual summer wear: t-shirts and wrap skirts. Julie, the new librarian, is there to show me what's changed in the past three years. The first thing I notice is that she's completely re-catalogued the book library. Using the Dewey Decimal System. "I hope you don't mind. I needed a bit of a challenge," she says. "So I thought I'd modernize things a little." I refrain from mentioning that Mr. Dewey was born in 1851.

"Having the same classification number for every book does look very modern," I say. "And lots easier to shelve them. If you make a mistake you're never very far off." Julie looks a little uncertain. As if she's not quite sure whether I'm complimenting her or telling her she's an idiot. I have learned a lot from business school, even though I'm only halfway through.

Don takes us out to lunch at our usual spot, Bersani & Carnevale on Avenue Road. He's in a great mood because he'll have no gap in librarian-ing while Julie is off work. "Why did they call it Avenue Road? Couldn't they decide which one it was? Why not Avenue Road Street?" he says, and laughs like that's the funniest thing he's ever said. It probably is. We order glasses of wine, except for Julie, and spaghetti carbonara. We dip crusty bread in oil and balsamic vinegar while we wait for our lunch. Julie is the exact opposite of me. She's tall, with blond hair in a well-constructed French twist. She has stereotypical librarian glasses, the kind that emphasize neither stupid questions nor talking above a whisper will be tolerated. She wears sensible pumps and a roomy maternity jumper over a white shirt. She also carries a purse. I do not own a purse and never have. This makes me carefree and artsy.

Don is busy trotting out stories about the old days. Stories I had no idea he knew. "Remember when you took off to Calgary with Bob?" he says. "What about all those lunches you, Mr. Bill, and Rodney used to have at the Blue Cellar Room? Gangsters hung around there, you know. I thought it was so hilarious when the operators found out it was you who mucked up the 1,2 password!" All of this is making Julie uncomfortable. I'm guessing I've been the ghost in her machine and now she thinks I'm back from the grave to reclaim my territory. "I told Joe to watch out for you," Don says. "This girl's going to have an MBA soon. She's going to kick your ass!" No worries, Julie. You do not know the lengths to which I went to ditch this job. This is just a marriage of convenience. Or maybe more like a summer fling. No harm, no foul, and maybe a few laughs.

I settle in to the summer job tedium. Mr. Bill still stomps around like a giant ogre, scaring the new hires. Don still reorganizes the parking spots every second Friday. The operators at the I/O window still hate me, even though there's been a thousand percent turnover since I last worked here, so none of them should even know who I am. But there is something new. Rodney is now in charge of a profit centre called DI Associates, which rents out programming time, internally and externally. "It's the wave of the future," Rodney says. "We have computer timesharing, why not programmer timesharing?" Everyone calls him Lady Di, based on his imperiously royal approach to doling out programmers' time. Clearly the penchant for nicknames hasn't changed.

I can still do the job with my eyes closed, but even better than getting paid for not doing very much, I have gained, in the parlance of B-school, a corporate sponsor. I can pilfer endless amounts of office supplies, but most importantly, I have a computer at my disposal. Or actually, six of them.

* * *

When second year starts, I decide to run for student council treasurer. In fact, a bunch of us decide to run. Practically my whole cohort of self-appointed in-crowd. If we get elected, we can use the Graduate Business Council office as our hangout. My campaign slogans for treasurer are "I will always remember to expire the prepaid rent" and "More beer for everyone." That's the thing about the GBC. We are in charge of collecting student fees and allocating them. I win in a landslide. It helped that nobody ran against me.

Michelle is the GBC president. She would have graduated last year except she took a term off. She was on the GBC last year too. Not only does she know how the GBC works, she knows how second year works. I and the rest of the new student council gather for our first meeting in our office, a room in the basement furnished with several filing cabinets, two sagging couches covered with beige chenille bedspreads, a desk, a phone, and a manual Remington typewriter. The bookshelf above the desk holds a complete set of required textbooks for second year and copies of all the yearbooks. There's also a bar fridge full of beer. "We have to sample it before we sell it," says Michelle. "Wouldn't want to sell bad beer. We could get sued."

Michelle calls the meeting to order. We go through the business at hand: the next pub night, the intramural sports schedule, forming a subcommittee to choose the venue for the Christmas dance. Then, Michelle gets up, pulls a ring full of keys out of her book bag, and opens the filing cabinet. "Gather 'round, kids," she says. "You are about to learn the secret of the archives. Otherwise known as the main reason you're on the GBC. Except you probably didn't know that." She lifts several thick file folders out of the drawer, passes them around, and tells us they are assignments from previous years.

She lets that sink in for a moment before going on to say there are three rules for accessing the archives. "First, you must pay it forward. A copy of your marked assignments must be submitted. Second, you can share the archives, but only with people you can personally vouch for. Third, nobody talks about the archives." Dave hands me one of the folders. It's full of Professor Graham's finance assignments from the past five years. I notice that each year, the topics are identical. I guess there aren't many things that could possibly change in finance from year to year. You always buy low and sell high, choose an appropriate discount rate, and expense your lunches.

Michelle tells us the textbooks above the desk have been highlighted to indicate the sections that are usually on the test and the sections that are relevant to the case studies. "These may not leave the room," she says, "but you are welcome to use them to highlight your own copy. It's all about collaboration. That's what they want us to do, after all." I'm not so sure about that, but since we still need to do the reading, prepare the assignments, and write the exams, there can't be anything really wrong with helping things along with info from the archives. "Use these as examples," she says. "They are only to give you an idea of what you need to do to get an *A* and what you should not do if you don't want a *D*. We're just taking a shortcut," she says. Like any good business person would do. Time is always of the essence when it comes to business. I also noticed there were no materials for MIS. I guess I'm on my own there.

* * *

1985

Every course in second-year business school involves group projects. To teach us how to problem solve in teams, just like we'll have to do in the real world. To teach us that everyone has strengths to bring to the table, just like we'll have to do in the real world. To teach us how to see the big picture, just like we'll have to do in the real world. In reality, this mostly serves to teach us how to backstab, blackmail, and bully, just like we'll have to do in the real world. The one saving grace is we can form our own groups. Or maybe it's not a saving grace because deciding who to align with is as dangerous and delicate as dismantling a timebomb. One wrong move and you're stuck in an explosive situation you can't get out of. None of the groups are accidental. There are the barracudas, a bunch of women who try to hide their razor-sharp teeth when they smile so you'll be surprised when they bite off your hand. Kind of hard to write an exam if that happens. There are the quantitative nerds, who think the HP12C is for preschoolers. They lug around the TI89, which uses reverse Polish notation. Whatever that is. The group I find myself in is like a collection of jewel thieves assembled to pull off the perfect heist. We have a specialist for everything. Martine knows the shortcuts for analyzing cases. Roger produces impeccable exhibits. Glen crunches numbers. Linda creates flawless marketing plans. Dave actually understands economics. I can type.

The strategy course is the capstone for the MBA program. We are supposed to use everything we have learned so far to analyze an industry and recommend a course of action that will help it increase profit, solidify its market domination, and/or improve its ability to pillage and plunder the planet. We meet once a week with the professor for an hour in the classroom. The rest of the time is devoted to our group project. In class, our focus is on assimilating the wisdom of Michael Porter's *Competitive Strategy* via a set of case studies that highlight strategies that have gone terribly wrong. The yacht builder that wrecked itself. The clothing company that could never quite fit in. The oil company whose fortunes dried up. I'm thinking this strategy stuff is clearly not for amateurs. I'm also thinking no industry in its right mind would hire students to dispense advice that, in all likelihood, will lead to its demise. But what do I know?

My group gathers in our usual corner of the Pits to throw around some ideas for which industry to choose. Roger knows the auto industry. Glen has a handle on banking. Martine has the inside scoop on the grocery business. I have a pretty good handle on how pizza delivery works. Sort of. At least I've ordered enough of them. We ultimately decide on grocery. We've all bought food. We've all eaten food. We've all read the flyers. We're all experts.

We divvy up the work to divide and conquer: Roger will do marketing, Glen will do finance, Martine will do logistics, Linda will do merchandizing, and I will handle management information systems and automation. I'm betting the barracudas would never divvy up work because each of them needs total control over everything.

* * *

I've done some research into point-of-sale systems, but I haven't found any sources with enough detail about how they actually work. Maybe they don't want to give away trade secrets, but it's interfering with the ability to write my section of the strategy paper. Leverage is good, according to the finance prof. Use other people's money. But leverage is not just about money, it works anytime you can use something to maximum advantage and minimal effort. It's time for me to do just that.

Mr. Bill is still in the office when I get there after class. I act nonchalant and extremely diligent as I move output binders around. This works like a charm. I hear Bill's boots approach my cube. "What's new in business?" he says. I tell him about MIS class and say I have gained new respect for Dataline's business model. Bill snorts. "'Business model.' You've sure got the lingo down, I'll give you that." I start reeling in my catch.

"Hey Bill, what do you know about point-of-sale software and hardware? Do we have any retail customers?"

This pulls Bill's string like he's a Chatty Cathy doll and he proceeds to give me a core dump. He talks nonstop for twenty minutes about the ins and outs of POS. Data transmission, data collection, barcode scanning, productivity, technology leverage. Leverage. Everything revolves around leverage. Wow. Even Bill knows about leverage. I scribble furiously in my school notebook. My section of the strategy paper will practically write itself, even without the archives.

* * *

We convene at the Pits to assemble our deliverable. That's what you call essays in B-school. There's a different word for everything, a tribal lexicon that only the initiated can understand. Roger commandeers a big table and takes his essay-assembly implements out of his Eddie Bauer knapsack. That's clearly going to have to be retired once he's a newly minted MBA, but for now it serves the right purpose. He has White-Out, glue sticks, a ruler, and a pad of graph paper. It looks like a Grade 3 art class.

We've arrived with our completed components. Roger will assemble the body, Linda will add the introduction and summary of recommendations, Martine will create the table of contents, and I will run a dozen copies and coil-bind them, courtesy of Dataline. Glen says with great gravitas, "Ladies and gentlemen, I think we have succeeded in plotting the course of the grocery store industry to meet the challenges of the 1990s and beyond. We've told them how to increase profit by selling more health and beauty products, how to decrease overhead by automating point-of-sale, and how to optimize product mix by analyzing customer buying habits. We are officially brilliant." I can't help but notice most of our strategy hinges on technology.

Roger is hunched over a blank page, positioning a hand-drawn graph in the centre. "Didn't you want me to generate those? It would look like we did tons of extra work if we could include printouts," I say.

"We have no time for that. It's due in two days," he says. "That would take at least two weeks."

"No it won't," I say. "Just give me all the charts and I'll run up the office right now. I'll be back in a couple of hours, max."

I ride my bike three blocks to Dataline and sit down at the terminal at my desk. I look at the blinking green cursor. All I need to do is type in some instructions at the command line. *Graph X Y, X=year, Y=dollars.* Then a delineated string of numbers. That's how simple DEC commands are. Then all I have to do is tell it to compute and print.

An hour later, I go upstairs to the I/O window and ring the bell. Dave's on duty today. Good thing. Dave actually doesn't hate me. "Dave," I say, "any way you can cut these down to letter size?" He nods and takes the sheaf of output to the paper guillotine. In one slash of the knife my printouts are now deliverable-ready.

Back at the Pits, Roger is still cutting and pasting. I hand him the stack of graphs and tell him to pop them in. No pasting necessary. I leave everyone to their remaining manual tasks. Computers may never save paper, but they sure save time. Maybe I'll go to a movie or grab dinner at Swiss Chalet or go for a run before I need to come back to start photocopying. But time saving is not a virtue in business school. Here, it's more important to talk about eighty-hour weeks and all-nighters and face-time. In the world of business, a tree only falls when there's somebody to see it.

11

My Second First Job

<u>1985</u>

There's a row of chairs in the hall outside the third-floor seminar rooms in the B-school building. I'm sitting on one of them, wearing my job interview uniform: a grey raw-silk jacket over a cream-coloured cotton blouse, with a stiff, discretely diamond-patterned, bow tied at the neck. My black blandly herringboned wool skirt ends just below the knee. I am telegraphing my studious adoption of *The Women's Dress for Success Book* by John Molloy. This is Mr. Molloy's attempt to expand his dress-code empire to include the other half of the population. His focus is on how executive women should dress so as not to offend the men they work with, yet still appear "feminine." I'm hoping my outfit will do the trick for the on-campus recruiters from IBM.

    I am summoned into the room, clutching my resume and my Day-Timer diary. There are two men at the table, indistinguishable from each other, with brush cuts, skinny ties, and white button-down shirts. I take my place in the hot seat. "Tell me about yourself," Guy A says. I launch into the interview version of my illustrious career, ending with how I ended up in this room. Waterloo. Toronto. Saskatoon. My triumph in New York. The two IBM emissaries nod in unison as they follow the bouncing ball of my success narrative. The easy part is over.

Guy B takes the reins. "What's your experience with the IBM 370?" he asks. I reiterate my computer science credentials from Waterloo, with maybe an over-confident emphasis on the extent of the IBM component of my education. "How long ago was that?" I admit it has been seven years since I touched the keyboard of an IBM terminal. Guy B makes a notation in his interview binder. "What about recently? Have you worked with computers recently?" This is the opening I've been waiting for. I proceed to recount my experience with Dataline's six DEC 10s, as one of the inner-circle entrusted with the sacred 1,2 password, my intricate task of uploading software revisions, and my familiarity with computer manuals. I leave out the part about how the operators hand down the fable of the tape-mounting terrorism to all new hires, to make sure the cautionary tale is perpetuated. The IBM twins write furiously as I finish my story. Guy B looks at his watch. "That's all the time we have," he says. "We'll be in touch about next steps."

Later in the week, Mrs. Webber, the B-school recruiting coordinator, posts the schedule for the next round of interviews. I have one with Imperial Oil. An oil and gas company. I don't even drive, and the last time I had even the slightest interest in oil and gas was ten years ago during the energy crisis, and that was only because it was on the geography exam. My name isn't on the IBM list. Only Steve, Rory, and Kevin. All guys.

I knock on Mrs. Webber's door. She favours vertically striped chunky sweaters in classic 1980s combinations of burnt orange, chocolate brown, sunflower yellow, and muddy green.

Her glasses hang from a chain around her neck, and her shoes are brown lace-up Wallabees, perhaps the ugliest shoes ever invented (the Earth shoe not withstanding). She cares about our success, not dressing for hers, nudging us like fledgling eagles out of the MBA nest toward the open sky of high-flying corporate careers. "Mrs. Webber," I say, "how come I'm not on the IBM next round interview list?"

She motions for me to sit and opens a leather-covered binder, embossed with *Class of 1985* on the spine in what is probably real gold, to consult her feedback notes. She tells me IBM thought I was very professional. (Thank you, bow tie.) They thought I was very knowledgeable about computers. Too knowledgeable. Too knowledgeable about the DEC 10, in particular. "Let me read to you what they said," she offers. "Our management training program takes smart people and turns them into true-blue IBMers. We find this works best if they come in as a blank slate. We know IBM has the best hardware and software on the planet. Maybe even in the universe. We made it possible to put a man on the moon, after all. We feel it would take too long to de-program this candidate from her exposure to the inferior DEC systems. We also think she might make the other trainees feel uncomfortable." Okay then. It was good that I know next to nothing about the IBM 370. It was bad that I know DEC machine language. And maybe also bad that I'm not a man. I smile at Mrs. Webber and tell her I'm looking forward to the Imperial Oil interview.

Same interview suit. Same interview room. Same resume. Two new and different identical interviewers. White shirts. Skinny ties. Slightly longer hair, but still short back and sides. There must be a *Dress for Recruiting Success* book out there somewhere. "Tell me about yourself," they say in unison. I pretty much have this down pat, except now I'm wary of saying too much about some things and not enough about others. I finish my school and work biography and wait for the hardball questions. Where do you see yourself in five years? Tell me about a time when you had to handle a difficult situation. If you were a tree, what kind of tree would you be? But none of these questions get asked. Instead, the duo launches into a monologue, trading turns every paragraph or so, about how wonderful Imperial Oil is (oil makes the world go 'round), how great the amenities are at headquarters (everyone gets their own office), and the opportunities for advancement and travel (Calgary! Halifax! Houston!). When they finish, they sit there beaming. Looking at me expectantly.

I make a show of opening my Day-Timer. "Well," I say, "it appears I have another appointment in five minutes. Is there anything else you need from me at the moment?" They tell me it was a pleasure meeting me and they'll be in touch. I hope not.

The next day, Mrs. Webber intercepts me in the hall after marketing class. "You have a job offer," she says. She scurries toward her office, glasses bouncing off the chest of her sweater, waving her arms wildly, beckoning me to follow her. She passes the photocopier in the admin office on the way and retrieves a document from the glass and one from the output tray. "I made a copy for my file. I keep them all so we can compare offers from year to year. It helps with negotiations," she says. Mrs. Webber has her own version of the archives! Michelle must be right. It is standard operating procedure. She hands me the offer letter. It's on Imperial Oil letterhead. Mrs. Webber is busy chattering away about what a good company it is and how anxious they are to hire more women. I stash the envelope in my book bag. I'll look at it later when I get home. After I spend a few hours at Dataline, hit the gym, grab something to eat, and hang out at Karen's to watch *Cheers*.

The cockroaches scatter when I open the door to my apartment and turn the light on. I always stand in the doorway for at least five minutes to give them lots of time to hide. They're out of sight but nowhere near out of mind. I pull off my cowboy boots and place them in a plastic bag, which I seal with an industrial strength twist tie. I keep my clothes in lidded plastic boxes stacked on top of upside-down milk crates. I don't keep food in the kitchen. I have never completely entered the kitchen since the day I moved in. My dishes, cutlery, and glassware have not been touched since then, and every second day, I fling a bunch of diatomaceous earth into the room. It's about two inches deep on all surfaces at the moment.

I take my book bag over to the pullout couch, releasing a cloud of eau-de-Raid as I sit to examine the job offer. It's surprisingly good. Imperial Oil wants to hire me to work in their information technology department. They are going to give me twenty-thousand dollars more than I was making in Saskatoon. Four weeks' vacation. A pension plan. A car allowance. Okay, maybe that part is kind of useless. But there's one small problem. The letter doesn't say exactly what my job will be nor my job title.

* * *

Tom meets me for lunch at an Italian restaurant on Yonge just north of St. Clair, near the office. He will be my boss if I decide to take the Imperial Oil job. "Call me Tom," he says when he phones to arrange our meeting. "None of this Mr. Franklin stuff." He's rumpled and apparently fond of tweed, and stands just half a head taller than me when I get up to shake his hand. He could not be less intimidating. When he called, he told me it's highly unusual that someone getting an MBA job offer would be assigned a specific job off the bat. "You drive a hard bargain," he said. "We had to go completely beyond protocol to place you in a position from day one." I replied that I found it highly unusual that someone would accept a job without actually knowing what the job is. "You're a smart cookie," he said. "That's why I wanted you in my group. That, and the fact I'm below my quota of women. You didn't hear me say that."

I'd already decided to take the job even though I didn't know what it was. Mrs. Webber told me the offer was extremely competitive and that I was unlikely to do better anywhere else. Worst case, stay a year or two and leverage myself into something better, she said. It's always about leverage, after all. Tom is describing what I'll be doing, while I fold my hands in my lap and adhere to the lunch-meeting etiquette we learned in our interview prep class. Do not eat anything messy. (A little hard to do when there's only pasta on the menu.) Do not pick up your fork until your host has done so. (No problem. Tom has already picked his up, and is waving it to emphasize his points.) Elbows off the table. (Our table for two will barely accommodate our plates, let alone my elbows.)

Tom tells me I will be a Client Support Centre analyst. I will help the IOL employees learn how to use their newly issued IBM AT personal computers. He throws in a few more acronyms and initialisms that do not mean anything to me. "You'll be at the bleeding edge of end-user computing. You'll learn everything there is to know about desktop computing and productivity applications. It's the wave of the future." Somehow, I always seem to end up being part of the wave, but luckily, I haven't managed to drown yet, nor bleed out. I think I might actually like this job. I wait until we finish our spaghetti and coffee is poured before I tell Tom I'd be happy to work with him. I don't mention I hate coffee, just in case that's a deal-breaker.

* * *

In my mind, the viaduct bridge that turns Bloor Street into Danforth Avenue is way in the east end, but it's really only three subway stops from Yonge or a ten-minute bike ride from Sherbourne and Carlton. I ride up the big hill on Broadview that rises up from the lake and offers an expansive vista of the Bay Street banking towers. I have cash for the first and last month's deposit on a new apartment in my pannier bag, along with my job offer, just in case there's competition. Lately, downtown landlords have been demanding key deposits and signing bonuses. Hopefully, word of this has not crossed over the Don Valley Parkway.

    I lock my bike to a parking meter that has a sticker on it showing a bike behind a red circle with a slash through it. It's the one meter that doesn't already have a bike attached to it. The apartment is above a storefront on the Danforth. There's a door at sidewalk level that opens to a steep stairway that smells of a mix of bleach and the pine air fresheners that hang from the rearview mirror of taxis. It's actually not that unpleasant. The landlord runs a mortgage company downstairs that's only open during the week from nine to five. His name is Ditmar and his English is tinged with his native German. He tells me he wants someone quiet and responsible, who can keep an eye on the office on the weekend and to take the licence plate number of anyone who parks illegally in the alley after hours. And the tenant needs to be clean. He does not want cockroaches. Neither do I, Ditmar.

We tour the suite: living room with a large window overlooking the street. An eat-in kitchen. A real bedroom! A sunroom at the back with a baseboard heater and a fire escape that leads down to the parking spaces. There's another room with a separate entrance that doesn't come with the rental, which Ditmar uses for storage. I can live with that, and also with the weird bathroom off the living area that has purple fixtures and lime green tile. Ditmar decides I will be the perfect tenant. I hand over my cash deposit, and just as I'm leaving, equipped with the paperwork I need to fill out, he asks me if I have a cat. I tell him I don't and do not plan to have pets, just in case he has a problem with that. "Too bad," he says. "Maybe you could get one."

* * *

Tom neglected to mention the Client Support Centre is a brand-new thing. Like, so new they've just finished constructing our work area. I do get the promised office with a door, but it's in the middle of a row of three inside offices that are enclosed in glass from chair-rail height to the ceiling. There's an open area with various printers, plotters, and microcomputers where staff can come and learn about the newfangled equipment. My office will be about as private as the information booth at Grand Central Station.

We're not exactly a profit centre, but we need to justify our existence based on how many "clients" we help and how happy they are. My very first task on my very first day is to help drum up business for our service. A service I only have a very tenuous grasp of. Tom takes me and my two fellow CSC analysts, Vince and Marge, on a dog-and-pony show to various conference rooms in head office and our satellite buildings. He has a dazzling deck of acetate slides full of facts about the value of personal productivity applications and service-level promises, and the crowds love it. After the third presentation, Tom decides we know the drill enough to go forth and continue the evangelism on our own.

I schedule my first solo tour down the street at Esso Chemical. Tom is right. I do know the drill. I flip the acetates like a pro, field all the questions, and pass out mugs with the CSC phone number. The meeting ends and I start gathering up my roadshow materials. All of the attendees have left the room except one, a guy who's hanging back, looking at me, clutching his freebie mug. "You're Marilyn Carr," he says.

"Yes, that's right," I say. "I just started. I'll be one of the people at the end of the phone when you call." I resume bundling the presentation stuff and retrieving extra handouts from the conference table. He continues standing right there. He looks like the typical Esso Chem engineer guy. Plaid short-sleeve shirt. Khaki pants. Nondescript. Dweeby.

"You know my friend Morris," he says. "I was best man at his wedding. I'm Sam."

I do not know how to respond to this. I have never heard of Sam. How has he heard of me? The Cat got married? Who did he marry? No wonder there's been radio silence. Phone silence too. But why is he hanging around with someone like Sam? Has he forsaken his downtown ways? I channel The Cat's poker face. "Nice to meet you, Sam," I say. "If you'll excuse me, I need to get back to my office. Staff meeting. See you around." Sam has still not moved. I walk past him and duck into the stairwell so I don't get stuck with him in the elevator. Typical Cat move. He's always skulking somewhere out there, and when I least expect it, he pounces.

12

Call Me

1985

My office is a computational cocoon. I have my very own IBM AT, which stands for advanced technology, proclaiming it as state of the art in desktop computing in 1985. It was released a year ago to much fanfare because it has 16MB of memory, twenty-five times the brain power of its predecessor, the IBM PC. The box that holds the innards is eight inches high and twenty inches wide and has two floppy disk drives located horizontally, one above the other, on the right-hand side. The floppy disks are five-and-a-quarter-inches square, consisting of a thin piece of plastic with a round cutout in the middle, which holds a thin, circular, magnetic disk. It looks kind of like a tiny forty-five RPM record in its sleeve, except that if you try to take the disk part of a floppy disk out of the protective cover, you ruin the disk. Floppy disks are not meant to flop about on their own. They need to stay in their straightjacket. The top disk drive can read supercharged 1.2MB disks, while the slot below is limited to 360KB, the previous maximum storage.

I have a multi-line telephone and an answering machine. Everybody in the company has an answering machine, which does away with the requirement for someone to intercept phone calls, take messages, and leave a trail of pink While-You-Were-Out slips. There's a central phone number for the CSC, which rings on each of the three CSC analysts' desks, bouncing from one to the other until it gets picked up. Apparently, our marketing efforts were successful because the phone buzzes constantly, except at 10:15 and 2:15, when the coffee-break ladies from the cafeteria arrive at the elevator rotunda with their carts, announcing themselves with clanging bells, a throwback to 1957 when the building opened. There are still pneumatic tubes that used to funnel inter-office mail from floor to floor.

The phones silence themselves for the duration of coffee break, but the open area of the CSC becomes an impromptu café, where folks gather to admire the new HP plotter and discuss last night's episode of *Dallas*. We encourage this, though, because every visitor counts in our usage statistics. If he could swing it, Tom would hang a sign over the door with one of those rolling tally counters like they have on the McDonalds' signs. "Over one million served," it will say, on the day he accepts the award for best nonprofit profit centre, in some imagined future. I'm glad I don't need to answer the phone during this brief respite. My neck is permanently cricked to the left. I'm busy complaining about this as I eat my raisin tea biscuit. Both Vince and Marge look at me with raised eyebrows, their necks exceedingly straight and supple. "Why not just use the speakerphone button?" Marge says. I tell her I prefer the more personal touch of talking into the receiver. When I go back to my desk, I see the button she means. The big red one. I've been afraid to push it in case it sets off the fire alarm or something. So that's why Vince can tilt back in his chair with his feet on the desk when he's answering calls. Not that he answers a lot of them. He's too busy bustling around, organizing the equipment, trying to look like he runs the joint and we're his minions.

The phones start ringing again at two thirty. I press the button beside the flashing light for the CSC line and greet the post-coffee caller. There is silence, then breathing. Heavy breathing. "Hello? Hello?" I don't want to drop a call. I have to record dropped calls and they count against our stats. More heavy breathing.

"I can see your juicy thighs," the caller says. "I'm running my hand up your skirt. I have my member in my other hand." I hang up. I look down at my skirt, expecting to see an arm protruding from the hem. I'm in one of those horror movies. The kind where the killer's call is coming from inside the house.

The next day, once the post-coffee-break phones resume ringing, a call bounces from Vince to Marge to me. I answer, my voice dripping with helpful reassurance. It's the breather again. I hang up. This happens every day for the next week. I'm not quite sure how to broach this subject with Tom. "Tom, is there a special statistics category for obscene callers? If not, I think we need one." "Tom, if I pick up a call and all I hear is heavy breathing, how long should I wait to make sure it's not just someone with asthma?" "Tom, in a company with two thousand employees, what percentage should we expect to be perverts?" Instead, I decide to do nothing except continue to hang up. I don't want to call attention to myself.

Tom calls an impromptu staff meeting during coffee break the following Monday. Maybe everyone else has been getting breathers too. But that's not the topic. Tom tells us we're going to offer in-person training for Lotus 123. Starting next Monday, we'll go on the road with portable computers and hit every satellite office in Eastern Canada. "Who wants to volunteer to go first?" he asks. Marge looks down at her pregnant stomach. Vince is suddenly very interested in his fingernails.

"I'll go," I say. This will get me away from the phones for at least five days, and maybe the breather will give up. There's only one small problem. I don't know how to use Lotus 123.

"Perfect," says Tom. "With your MBA you must already be a spreadsheet whiz. You'll leave on Sunday."

* * *

My new Danforth apartment is furnished with the finest specimens Honest John's Used Furniture had to offer. The store is just two doors down the street from me, and they agreed to deliver everything for free, even up the steep stairs: a walnut dining room set from the 1920s, and a sensuously curved couch and chair set from the 1930s that got recovered along the way in burnt-orange velvet, exactly the same colour as the fireplace I had on Bedford Road. As if to prove its point, the chair has a few cigarette scars on the right arm just above the carved wood trim. My only nod to anything post-war is the two pink plastic flamingos installed in the front window in the gap between the glass and the screen. Carefree. Artsy.

I'm hosting a dinner party tonight to celebrate my new digs and also the fact I now have a kitchen I'm willing to enter. There will be spinach salad with strawberries and goat cheese, chicken cutlets in a white wine beurre blanc reduction, and profiteroles smothered in chocolate sauce for dessert. But first I need to hit the fruit market. I check the weather in the flamingos' front yard. Spitting October rain. Rather than get a fresh pair wet, I rummage through my dirty laundry basket to retrieve yesterday's jeans and a DayGlo-pink t-shirt with a cartoon cow on the front wearing a straw hat and sunglasses, souvenir from a bike trip I took to Vermont. I shove my bare feet into an elderly pair of Birkenstocks, grab my keys and yellow rubber anorak, and head out the door just as the rain lets loose.

It's Saturday, so despite the weather, the Danforth is hopping and bopping with baby strollers double-parked in front of the bookstore, and coffee wanderers huddled underneath the restaurant awnings. The Chinese fruit and veg mart at the corner of Logan has umbrellas over the stalls that line the sidewalk, to shelter the people elbowing each other to get to the out-of-season berries and weird looking root vegetables rejected by the corporate grocery store buyers. I locate the strawberries, some spinach, and a bunch of dill, and line up to pay. I heft my plastic bag and cross the street to head back west, the weight of the handles creating welts on my palms. The rain has slowed to a trickle but I'm still drenched. I'm almost home when someone taps me on the shoulder. Maybe I forgot to take my change. I stop and turn toward the tap.

"This guy thinks he knows you," says the tapper, a tall, bearded, artsy man. I look in the direction he's pointing, toward another bearded, artsy man. The Cat.

"I do know her," The Cat says. "Imagine running into you here." I stand on the sidewalk in yesterday's jeans, stringy hair in my eyes, wondering whether the manhole cover a few feet away could manage to open up and swallow me. "Come and have a beer with us," he says. I lift up my grocery bags and say I need to put them away. "Go ahead and do that," he says, as he glances up to my flamingos. "We'll wait for you at the Willow." While they continue down the block to the bar, I start weighing the pros and cons.

The cons are still yammering in my ears as I wash the spinach, cut up the strawberries, take the chicken out to thaw, set the table, examine the cleanliness of the wine glasses, make the batter for the profiteroles, and locate the candles. Then the pros intensify their side of the argument. Who the heck did he marry? How does he know where you live? Is he the obscene caller? I change into fresh cords and a purple silk shirt. I shrug on a beaded jean jacket and jam my feet into my pink cowboy boots. I tie a darker pink bandana on my wet head, entirely encompassing my hair like a biker chick. My boots lead me downstairs, out the door, in the direction of the Willow.

The Cat and his friend are three-quarters of the way through a pitcher of draft. Since lunch is long over and it is way early for dinner, there's hardly anybody in the bar. The Mariachi music has nothing to drown it out. "This is my friend Sam," The Cat says, shouting over the Mexican soundtrack. "That took a while. Do you live far from here? I thought you'd run away again." I can completely imagine the conversation I've missed. A continuation of the constant chatter about me that's been humming in the background for years, unbeknownst until Sam made that fact apparent. Sam gets up abruptly, winks at me, and says he has to go, as he hurries toward the door. The Cat looks at me with his heavily lidded eyes and blinks slowly. He's wearing a shiny gold wedding ring. I wave to the bartender to bring over another glass. I say nothing as I pour myself some flat beer, spilling some on the front of my expensive yuppie blouse, swearing under my breath.

We sit and say nothing for a while. He's playing the boardroom legal-suit settlement game: whoever speaks first loses. He's probably forgotten I'm familiar with this tactic. He told me about it a few years ago, while trying to impress me with his newly acquired lawyering skills. I'll admit I was impressed. I'll also admit I lose every time. This is no exception. I stand up and say I have to leave because I'm having people over for dinner. "You can't leave," he says. "You just got here. We have lots to catch up on." Right then, the bartender shows up with a bottle of champagne. Already open. "See? It would be a shame to let this go to waste." He has a point. Lawyers are masters of getting their way.

The restaurant starts to fill up, so it must be getting late. I have guests arriving at six thirty. I tell The Cat I really do need to get home. He nods, grabs his coat off the back of the chair, and we walk out. For the past hour and a half, we spoke of nothing consequential. Hot new restaurants. Trends in litigation. The collapse of the dollar. All the while, The Cat waved his left hand around, literally shoving the wedding ring in my face. I did not get answers to any of my questions, likely because I did not ask any of my questions. He hands me his card and I shove it in my pocket. Seems rude not to. "Call me," he says.

"Give my regards to Sam," I say. Let him figure that one out. I guess I'm serving pizza tonight.

* * *

The train pulls into Sarnia on Sunday afternoon. Downtown Sarnia is three blocks long, with an Eaton's store at one end, a movie theatre at the other, and the usual scattering of greasy spoons, used appliance stores, and beauty parlours in between. The skyline consists of the oil refinery smokestacks, evidently the only things working today except maybe the one taxi outside the station door. I bundle my bag into the back seat and ask the driver to take me to the Delta Hotel. He puts down his Sunday *Sun*, and grunts like this is an inconvenience. I guess it is, if the highlight of your news consumption is the Sunshine Girl. He grinds the shift into drive and does a three-pointer so the cab faces downhill toward the river, and drives half a block to a building right behind the tracks, hidden by the slope of the riverbank. Delta Hotel, it says. "The minimum's three bucks," he says. I hand him a five and wait for change. I will not give him a tip for a three-second ride. My travel per diem is fifteen dollars without receipts. My plan is to spend as little as possible, charge full amount on the expense report, and pocket the rest. I didn't go to business school for nothing. I check in to the hotel, grab a couple of apples from the fruit bowl at the reception desk, and go up to my room. My version of room service dinner. Twelve bucks destined for my wallet already.

I read the Lotus 123 instruction manual on the train, so I'm at least a few pages ahead of my students. When I arrive at the Sarnia office conference room early Monday morning, there's a coffee urn and a plate of muffins and Danishes on the credenza. My plan to eat for free is falling into place. The eight portable computers shipped ahead from Toronto are lying in the corner, looking less functional than an electronics junkyard. Weighing almost thirty pounds, and about the size of a sewing machine, the Compaqs are better described as luggable than portable. A full-size keyboard detaches from the long edge of the metal cabinet to reveal a six-inch-square green display screen, which shows the ghosts of spreadsheets past, a hazard of leaving the screen on too long. As in for more than twenty minutes. There's 128KB of memory, or roughly one-sixth of the capacity of the disk drives, and no hard drive, hence the need to boot them from a floppy. They are the computer equivalent of an Easy-Bake Oven. Functional only if you've never used the real thing.

I heft the computers on to the conference table and ready them for action like a NASA control centre commander preparing for liftoff. Keyboard detached: check. Power supply attached: check. Power switch activated: check. Flashing power light verified: check, check, check, check, check, check, check, crap! I guess I don't get a computer. I may have read the manual, but I have never actually touched the software. Too late now. Boot disks loaded: check. Boot sequence initialized: check. Flashing cursors: check. Lotus 123 logo display: check. Showtime.

My eight students shuffle in, looking apprehensive. Suddenly I feel like I'm a hundred pages ahead in the manual instead of one. I'm a microcomputer rocket scientist and spreadsheet wizard next to these guys. I launch into my spiel. "Lotus 123 has 2,048 rows and 256 columns, so each spreadsheet can hold more than 500,000 cells of data," I read from my cheat notes. "We're going to learn how to create and enter formulas, copy and paste cells, and print. Well, not really print because we don't have a printer, but we can pretend print. Sort of. Okay, never mind about printing. Let's pretend it's a paperless office."

I give everyone their student manual and exercises, and settle in to eat a muffin. I can use my time to calculate how much money I'll have at the end of a week of not paying for food. Except that nobody has started to do anything. They're just staring at the keyboard. The guy with the tent-card that says Jim puts up his hand. "How do you use this typewriter thing?" The other students look relieved. Jim has put their dread into words. Forget about spreadsheets, they need to go all the way back to keyboarding 101. And I'm exactly the right person to take them there. I am the proud owner of a high school certificate that says I can type one hundred words a minute. Something to fall back on, if need be. That need is now.

"Okay," I say. "Put your index fingers on the *F* and *J* and your other three fingers on the rest of the row. Your thumbs will work the space bar." Then I realize practically all they'll need to do is use the number, brackets, and arithmetic symbols. "Scratch that," I say. "See that set of keys on the right that looks like a calculator? See the symbols on top of the numbers? Let's practice with those."

By the time our sandwiches arrive at noon, I have a room full of nascent keyboard jockeys, and I'm now the equivalent of two hundred pages ahead in the manual because I only have to shepherd them through half a day of actual spreadsheeting. The afternoon passes without incident, as my students begin coaxing their cells to add, subtract, multiply, and divide. At four thirty, I announce we'll reconvene at eight the next morning, and my star pupils beam as they pack up to leave. Even better, there are still two sandwiches left. This will be a full fifteen-dollar day. But it's not over yet. I grab a bun filled with egg salad and sit down at one of the Compaqs and turn to the first page of the student guide. I need to become a spreadsheet ace before sunrise.

13

Send in the Clones

<u>1986</u>

My biz school pals and I have started an investment club. We've opened a trading account and each ponied up a stake. We are each responsible for selecting a stock, accompanied by substantial research and exhibits to support our recommendation. I thought I was done with finance fire drills. I guess not. I'm mostly in the club to drink wine and eat hors d'oeuvres once a month. But the fact remains that these things do not come without picking a stock. This month, I have selected Lotus Corporation. When it came out in 1983, Lotus 123 toppled VisiCalc like the iceberg squashed the *Titanic*. "It's a killer app," I tell my fellow fledgling investors.

"What's a 'killer app'?" Martine says.

"It's like a category killer," I say. "Everybody wants Lotus 123 so much that computers that don't run it are toast. I think soon it will ship with every IBM and compatible. And everyone will have to pay for upgrade releases every year. They won't want to be left still wearing Levi's when everyone else has moved on to Tommy Hilfiger's."

"Now that I understand," says Martine. "I move we buy one hundred shares.

"But aside from the continued market domination, what we really want is a takeover. That's all any tech company is in business for. To be acquired."

"How do you know this?" says Martine.

"Osmosis. Dataline." I'm discovering more and more that my first job was not a total waste of time.

* * *

The air in my apartment smells stale when I get home from another Lotus 123 road trip, but there's also whiffs of other things: the tang of sweet and sour chicken balls rising up from the Chinese restaurant next door, the acrid stench of coffee beans being roasted at the café on the corner, and an undertone of cat pee, which is impossible because, despite Ditmar's wish, I do not have a cat. At least not the four-legged kind. I open the windows to let the April breeze freshen things up, while I sit on the couch to sort through the mail. As I thumb through the bills, junk food coupons, and Publishers Clearing House envelopes that say I may have already won a few million dollars, I notice something out of the corner of my eye. Something moving in the kitchen. I look up and see nothing. It must have been the wind in the curtains. I go back to the electricity bill, reading the insert that tells me the rates are going up. It's the same insert every month. They could save paper by only including the insert if the rates aren't going up. Maybe the rates are going up because of all the paper they use. I add that to my list of reasons why the paperless office will never exist, chuck the junk mail in the bin I keep by the door, and when I turn around to go into the kitchen, I catch a glimpse of the source of the movement. A grey mouse tail disappearing beneath the stove.

I spend the next half-hour wondering how long I can last without ever going into the kitchen again. It worked okay on Sherbourne Street. If I get Chinese takeout, I could eat right out of the containers and avoid having to get a plate out of the cupboard. Except I'll still need to put the leftovers in the fridge. The biggest problem, though, is that I have to go through the kitchen to get to my bedroom. But wait, I can always sleep on the couch! That would work. But after another half-hour, I realize if I am going to continue to pretend to be a grown-up, I need to take control of this situation.

I order Cantonese chow mien from the restaurant next door, and while I wait for it to be ready, I visit the hardware store down the street. Mr. Shewchuk, who owns the store, is about a thousand years old and so is most of his merchandise. Good thing nobody's improved on the mousetrap since then. I bring a single trap up to the front counter and fish a dime out of my pocket. "You're going to need more than one of those," Mr. Shewchuk says. Mr. Shewchuk, who carries every year of his acquired wisdom on his face, is the kind of man who wears a belt and suspenders. I tell him I only saw one mouse, so I'll just take the one. He rolls his eyes but takes my dime and puts it in the drawer of a cash register that's almost as old as he is.

I wake up to a sharp, snapping noise at three in the morning. Ding, dong, the mouse is dead. That wasn't too hard! I decide the burial can wait until a decent hour. When it's light, I put on my housecoat and a pair of knee-high rubber boots to survey the carnage. The mouse is indeed dead. Decapitated, even. The force of triggering the trap has moved it partially under the fridge. When I shift the appliance away from the wall, I'm hit with an onslaught of pee smell. It has crystalized on the floor underneath the cooling coils. Mouse pee, not cat pee. How could one mouse possibly pee so much? There is only one right answer to that question.

Mr. Shewchuk smiles an I-told-you-so as I pile ten traps on the counter and peel a dollar out of my wallet. "A dollar a dozen," he says. "You can get two more." This had better be a lifetime supply, Mr. Shewchuk.

* * *

The IBM AT is such a success it has spawned clones. The clones are computers that walk like an AT and speak fluent DisplayWrite and Lotus 123, but do not carry three blue initials nor the associated price tag. After extensive testing, Imperial Oil has decided all new desktop computer purchases will be Zeniths. Like the television. Or more accurately, like the assemble-it-yourself electronics from Healthkit, which has recently been bought by Zenith. This spawns many bad jokes. "How many CSC analysts does it take to put a Zenith together? Four. Too bad there's only three of them." "What do you get free with every Zenith? An electronics degree. You'll need one." "Do you know you can run a spreadsheet and watch *As the World Turns* at the same time on a Zenith? No, but if you hum a few bars, I can fake it."

Eighty new Zeniths arrived this week. My IBM AT has been swapped out for a Zenith because I'm in charge of troubleshooting in case there are problems. For a few weeks it's business as usual. I field calls about printers that won't print, spreadsheets that don't add up, documents that are illiterate, and am on the receiving end of a handful of breathers, or maybe several instances of the same breather. Hard to tell. I have indeed created my own stats column for them (him?). I plan to present it at our next quarterly all-hands IT department status meeting, complete with analysis charts generated from Lotus 123, and a frequency graph showing the most common creepy come-ons: "What are you wearing?" takes the prize. I will say I'm looking for much more innovation in the next quarter, maybe something along the lines of "Does my Zenith make you hot?" That should shake things up a bit.

But that's just the calm before the tsunami. This morning my phone lights up like a Broadway marquis, with dozens of panicked callers who say their disks have self-destructed and their files have fled. It's an utter computer calamity. A Zenith computer calamity. My very own calamity. Tom runs in and waves frantically at my cubicle window. "Quick," he says. "The executive floor called me personally. Something about losing the spreadsheets for the annual report." Okay, not just a calamity, a high-profile, potentially career-boosting calamity. Unless it's a career-limiting one.

I tell Tom I'll get right on it, locate my suit jacket, walk briskly to the elevator, and press the button for the twenty-first floor, a penthouse that apparently has views all the way to the lake. The door opens to face a large reception desk, which also acts as a security checkpoint for the inner sanctum. There are three Group of Seven prints on the wall above the receptionist's head. Tom Thomson's trees, Fred Varley's rainstorms, Lawren Harris's icy landscapes. I've seen them many times on greeting cards. A plush grey carpet muffles the clack of my kitten heels. The woman at the desk looks up from the notes she's taking in her steno pad. She looks like she just got back from the salon, with fresh frosted tips in her hair and a hint of baby-blanket pink on her manicured nails. I hide the ragged cuticles of my well-toothed fingers behind my back. "And you are?" she says.

I explain I'm from the CSC and I've come about the diskette problems. She glances at her appointment book and looks back at me. "Right," she says. "I'll take you to Miss Reed's desk. Do not go anywhere unless you are escorted. Do not speak unless spoken to. Do not take anything from this floor unless it has been signed out by me." At that moment, I notice the Group of Seven "prints" each have their own security camera and possibly invisible laser-beam alarms, like in those museum heist movies. I'm surprised I don't need to be fingerprinted. Not so far, anyhow.

Miss Reed has a huge office that interconnects with her boss's suite, the vice president of finance. She has about a dozen floppy disks strewn across her desk, some of which are lying there naked, without their jackets. Miss Reed is not in a happy place. I'm guessing her boss is in an order-of-magnitude unhappier one. "Mr. Wilson insisted I switch to a Zenith. He said it's our responsibility to be role models for fiscal frugality. Have you seen the price of oil lately? It's in the toilet." She bustles into his office and comes out seconds later. "He must have stepped out to the bathroom." I imagine a gold key, an executive comfort station replete with hot-and-cold running champagne, men in tuxes handing out warm sandalwood-scented hand towels, and if Miss Reed is right, toilet tanks filled with high-test gasoline. I hear a faint flush, then Mr. Wilson emerges from his doorway. Mr. Wilson has his own bathroom! Forget about stock options, I have now found my new goal: to be first in my MBA class to have a private privy.

Even though Mr. Wilson has not yet spoken to me, I risk contravening the receptionist's rule, and employ my soothing CSC hotline voice to tell him I'll need to take away the defective diskettes to try and retrieve the files with our recovery software. I put Miss Reed's Zenith on a trolley and tell her I'll give her mine instead. I know there's definitely nothing wrong with mine.

* * *

My answering machine light is flashing. It's a message from Ditmar. He's turning the storage room at the top of the stairs into office space. But first, there'll be a little renovation. It shouldn't bother me, he says, because they'll only be there during work days. I check my trapline. There have been fewer and fewer mice. I've only been back to Mr. Shewchuk's five times.

On Monday, when I arrive home after work, the stairs to my apartment are covered in plaster dust. I pass Ditmar's workmen leaving as I go up. They tell me they'll be finished in two days. "We're just putting a skylight in," a dark-haired guy says. "We covered the opening with plywood. It shouldn't be a problem." I've taken to keeping a keen eye on the rodent activity in the kitchen as I do my after-work puttering, leafing through the September *Toronto Life*, contemplating new upholstery for the hideous orange chair, and anticipating The Cat's next stealth attack. I don't see any sign of mice. But I do see something. It's on the wall, right beside my Monet poster. A cockroach.

I stomp downstairs to Ditmar's office. He waits politely as I rant about mice and plaster dust and cockroaches. He says he'll look into it. Ditmar says he's pretty sure the cockroaches have come from the restaurant next door. Once the ceiling got opened up for the skylight, they could come and go with abandon. "Perhaps you should get some diatomaceous earth in the meantime. It should be fine once everything is closed in," he says. *Perhaps I should move*, says my inside voice. *I could buy a house.*

I slam my way out the front door and stomp up the block to Mr. Shewchuk's. Like a barista who has your latte on the counter before you've barely crossed the threshold, he reaches under the counter for the stash of mousetraps he keeps handy for me. "Diatomaceous earth," I say. A phrase I thought I would never need to utter again.

* * *

My very own house is just over the Don Valley in Cabbagetown on Seaton Street. It's a three-storey row house that was built at the turn of the century. It has a gabled slate roof and Victorian exterior, but the inside has been transformed in spectacular 1980s fashion: glass blocks, sunken bathtub, skylit solarium, and a concept so open there are three doors in the entire house (including on two of the three bathrooms — don't ask) and a vertiginous sightline from the third-floor master suite all the way down to the finished basement. Everything is off-white. Walls, carpet, fixtures, kitchen.

The real estate agent said I got a steal of a deal. It was featured in the home section of the *Toronto Star* four years ago. "An architect owned it," he said. "This is a one of a kind." He also said I should get someone to look at the fridge. "I noticed it's making a weird noise. Maybe you'll need to buy a new one." This advice came only after I had signed the final papers and committed myself to a six-figure mortgage that starts with a two. But apparently, this is what it costs for a cockroach-free life in the city. And, if the real estate agent is to be believed, apparently it was a bargain.

The moving-in process was very smooth because I am a grown-up and can hire movers rather than pay beer and pizza to some reluctant friends. Good thing, too, because the reluctance factor would have increased ten-fold once they found out the house has four levels. But now the boxes have been emptied and my sparse furniture highlights the enormity of the space. I do not know what I was thinking. My bedroom is bigger than the entirety of every apartment I have ever lived in. Surely I don't deserve this, but I'll try to get used to it.

There's a message on my machine when I get home. My very first new-house phone call. On my very new phone number. It's from Ditmar. "Did you leave something behind?" he says.

I phone him back in the morning. "Ditmar, I made sure to check all the closets and cupboards. I can't think of anything I might have forgotten."

Ditmar pauses and clears his throat a few times. "In the sunroom," he says. "On the baseboard heater. There was a six-foot-long boa constrictor."

And I thought the arrival of the cockroaches were my worst problem. Maybe that explains the absence of mice. "Not mine, Ditmar," I say. "Maybe it's from the restaurant next door. Maybe you should get some diatomaceous earth." I admire my off-white enclave, as angular and haughty as a modern art museum. I am in a calm, secure, cocoon. Nothing can touch me here.

* * *

It's almost midnight and I'm still at work. The Zenith I substituted for the one on the executive floor is acting up and more and more people are reporting losing data. I need to produce a report on what I've done to try and solve the problem. The problem is diskettes are getting corrupted. The problem is I have not been able to recreate the problem. The problem is it only happens when I'm not there. I sat beside Miss Reed for a solid week and everything worked just fine. The minute I got back to my desk, her diskettes started to go bad. I have swapped out every moving part and even the ones that don't move. The motherboard. The monitor. The memory chips. The keyboard. Nothing made any difference. I feel like Wile E. Coyote trying to catch the Road Runner, and we all know how well that worked out. My little parasol is no match for the Zenith CPUs that are being launched at my head. But the subway will stop running soon. I have five minutes to determine my next step. The only thing I haven't tried is going through the IBM and Zenith manuals side by side. I guess that's what I'll do. Either that or go looking for a bottomless canyon to throw myself into.

By lunch the next day, I'm midway through reading the manuals but so far there are no obvious differences or, more importantly, none that aren't immediately obvious. I've just finished my tuna sandwich when I reach the section that describes the floppy drives. I am very aware that both the IBM and the Zenith have two floppy drives: one high-density that uses 1.2MB diskettes and one double-density that uses 360KB diskettes. Both manuals explain that you should not mix up your diskettes because the disk drive cannot detect whether it is reading a high-density or double-density diskette. Wait. What? The IBM manual has a section at the bottom of the page surrounded by exclamation marks encased in red diamonds. It says: *Use of a 1.2MB disk in the 360KB drive will not provide enough magnetization to correctly read the disk. Use of a 360KB disk in the 1.2MB drive will render it unreadable in the 360KB drive.* I flip to the same page in the Zenith manual. It has a section at the bottom of the page surrounded by exclamation marks encased in red diamonds. It says: *Use of a 1.2MB disk in the 360KB drive will not provide enough magnetization to correctly read the disk. Use of a 360KB disk in the 1.2MB drive will render it unreadable in the 360KB drive.* So much for that as the explanation. There should be no difference between what might go wrong with the IBM's drives and the Zenith's. And nobody is reporting problems with the IBM.

I gather up some fresh high- and double-density diskettes and head to the CSC lab, where I can line up an IBM next to a Zenith to see what happens if I use the wrong disk in the wrong slot. I've never looked at them this closely side by side before. There was no point. They're called clones for a reason: they look identical except for the logos. But then I notice something. They aren't completely identical. The IBM has an asterisk moulded into the faceplate of the lower, 360KB drive. The Zenith has two smooth faceplates, one below the other. The IBM reminds the user which disk drive is which. The Zenith does not. My week with Miss Reed was an exercise in the Hawthorne effect. I was watching her so she was extra careful.

The Zenith problem is fixed. All it took was an adhesive label on the 360KB drive. The problem with the oil industry is not fixed. The price of crude has fallen sixty percent. The Group of Seven paintings are worth more than what's coming out of the Alberta oil derricks. Business school taught us to follow the money. Maybe I should try banking.

* * *

1987

Mrs. Webber opens a binder labelled "Banking and Finance." One value-add of being a U of T B-school graduate is that we can use the placement office in perpetuity. They want to keep the alumni employment statistics robust. "Any particular bank," she asks. I tell her all I care is that it's on the subway. "Call this recruiter," she says. "Tell him I sent you. Here's a copy of the job requisition." The paper she hands me says "Manager, Management Information." Bingo.

I use Mrs. Webber's phone to dial the recruiter's number. I would not want to be caught doing this at work. Who knows how they might be monitoring our calls. I also use Mrs. Webber's machine to fax him my resume and agree to meet him on Friday afternoon.

My grey suit makes its requisite appearance at the appointed hour. The recruiter looks like a used-car salesman, in his green plaid jacket, cuffed brown pants, and point-toed brown lizard shoes. He tells me my credentials are perfect. "We don't get many people with both library and financial experience," he says. We run through the usual "tell me about yourself" stuff, and then move to the next step. "The bank takes fiduciary responsibility very seriously," says the recruiter. "Your background must be unimpeachable. That's why it has been tough to find a successful applicant. You'll need to fill in this questionnaire." He hands me what looks like an exam booklet. "Get it back to me by the end of the week. Time is of the essence." I get the feeling that it's the recruiter's commission that's of the essence. But I have nothing to hide, and I'm sure working with money rather than oil will be much more up my alley.

14

Show Me the Money

<u>1987</u>

I have joined the Home Service Club. This is a service for hapless homeowners like me, who need people to fix stuff that's broken. I maintain that I am not completely hapless. As proof, I have a one-size-fits-all adjustable wrench, where you manipulate a truncated abacus thing with your thumb to make it fit the dimension of the screw. Or maybe it's for bolts. I also have a screwdriver with interchangeable heads that live in the blue plastic see-through handle. Sometimes the Robertson piece (see? I even know what a Robertson is) stays in position for about three seconds before it falls off and rolls under the stove. This is usually right before all ten of the other screwdriver-drivers fall out of the handle and clatter down the heating vent. Lefty loosey, righty tighty. I know my stuff. But I don't know why the fridge is still making that weird noise.

The HSC refers me to Mr. T appliance repair. The significance of the name of this business does not occur to me until I open my door to a large Black guy who is bald, except for a sculpted mohawk, and sporting a massive collection of gold chains and pendants around his neck. I usher him in to the kitchen, which accounts for the first hundred dollars of his fee, suppressing my laughter as much as I can. Which is not very much. But I do not quibble about the cost. I am already thinking of ways in which I can dine out on this story. I retreat to the living room to let Mr. T do his magic. I have barely cracked open this month's *Chatelaine* magazine when he announces he has solved the problem. I am delighted I don't have to fork out for a new fridge.

Back in the kitchen, Mr. T explains the source of the problem. He uses short sentences and simple words. "This here thing at the bottom of the fridge is called a drip tray." He pauses a moment to make sure I am following the bouncing ball. "It's here to catch condensation. You can pull it out to clean it." He shows me how the tray slides out along lips mounted on each side of the bottom of the appliance. "If you don't put it back correctly, it will vibrate whenever the fridge comes on. And it will make a noise." Mr. T looks at me meaningfully, with a mixture of sorrow and superiority, picks up his unused toolkit, and hands me the top copy of a three-part invoice. Another hundred bucks. For five minutes work. Maybe I should switch from IT to appliance repair. I escort him to the front door. I can already imagine how many times he will dine out on this story. Me, not so much. Pity the fool.

* * *

The Office of the Chairman is on the twenty-fourth floor of Commerce Court North. It's an Art Deco skyscraper that was the tallest building in the British Commonwealth until the early 1960s. There are sixteen giant disembodied heads ringing the top, like a platoon of Ozymandias's emissaries surveying the magnificence of the banking district. Or maybe more like a phalanx of Easter Island effigies, marooned on a sandstone mountainside. The Office of the Chairman is the most important department in the bank's headquarters. Or at least that's what Rick, my new boss, says. "You are lucky to be here," he says. "And you must deport yourself with decorum at all times. Do not enter the elevator unless you are wearing a suit jacket. Do not enter the elevator if the chairman is in the elevator. Do not look at anyone in the elevator. Do not each lunch at your desk. Do not eat anywhere except the employee cafeteria. Do not eat anything with garlic. Do not chew gum. Do not do anything you should not." Well, I guess this will turn out to be a warm and fuzzy place. I'm pretty sure we won't be wearing cowboy boots in solidarity with Stampede week.

There was a joke making the rounds when we were in the midst of on-campus recruiting at business school. A newly minted MBA, having died of exhaustion, arrives at the gates of Heaven. There's a long line, and before he reaches the pearly gates, the Devil shows up and starts talking to him. "You don't look like the type that would like Heaven," he says. "It's no fun. It has none of the excitement of business school. While you're waiting, why don't you drop down and see what I have to offer?" The MBA thinks about this for a minute, and remembers the advice from the recruiting office: always keep your options open. He agrees and follows the Devil down to the gates of Hell. The Devil opens the door to a lavish party, with caviar, champagne, lobster, and prime rib. The partygoers all look like movie stars and are dripping with diamonds and gold jewellery. The Devil says "We have a different theme every day. Tomorrow is Hawaiian luau, Friday is casino night, and Saturday is all-you-can-eat sushi." The Devil gives him a tour of the living quarters, the gym, the yacht club, and the golf course. The MBA is very impressed. He tells the Devil he'll go back up to Heaven to tell them he's not coming.

When he returns to Hell, he is led through a rusty, barbed-wire gate, into a dim room where people dressed in rags are shovelling coal into a furnace. The MBA is incredulous. "What happened to all the partying and opulence?" he says to the Devil. The Devil smiles and replies, "Oh. That was when we were recruiting you." I have a sneaking suspicion I'm going to have flames nipping at my heels soon.

My new job is to oversee the preparation of the bank's monthly business performance briefing book that goes to the chairman and the executive vice presidents. It's a physical book, twenty-five Cerlox-bound copies. My mission is to automate it. Right now, it takes six weeks to pull the book together, which means the executives are always a month and a half behind in the important task of making sure the money keeps making more money. I need to shrink the gap down to two weeks, which cannot be done without considerable electronic muscle.

There is a new thing called Executive Information Systems. The next, new office automation wonder, which will save time and money, as long as I can convince a bank with endless funds that time is worth saving, since Rick's entire department only exits because lots of time is required to crank out the monthly briefing book.

For now, I'm learning the manual processes so I understand how it's done. My job boils down to bugging people to get their calculations finished, gathering spreadsheet files, generating graphs, cutting and pasting. The exact kind of job that requires an MBA.

Rick insists the final product must be flawless. "The executives are very particular," he says. "We do not want to offend them." Yes, sir. Three bags full, sir. Rick has selected the incorrect nickname for Richard. He's always rushing around like the White Rabbit, sneering at underlings and sucking up to his superiors. I guess this is what's required to be upwardly mobile at this bank. Any tarot card reader could accurately predict my future success. I have drawn the Devil.

* * *

The document production facility is in the sub-basement of the building. There's a long grey cinder-block corridor leading to a noisy room full of photocopiers, binding equipment, and industrial paper cutters. I deliver this month's book to the foreman, along with my requisition for twenty-five bound copies. He tells me it will be ready in two hours. "Office of the Chairman," he says. "The most important job we ever get." I go back up to my desk to wait.

"What are you doing up here?" yells Rick. "Do not let the book out of your sight! You must carefully observe each and every page as it leaves the photocopier! There might be a smudge!" I dash back down to the sub-basement. The photocopy person has already completed two copies, so I sit down to scrutinize the level of perfection. Looks good to me.

When the books are all finished and boxed, I take them upstairs and put them on Rick's desk. That's that for March. Tomorrow we start on April. I start packing up my stuff. "Not so fast," says Rick. "I have not yet reviewed the books. If there are quality errors, they will need to be corrected before tomorrow." I unpack my stuff. I look out the window toward Bay Street, watching the office towers empty out with people rushing to catch the commuter train.

I busy myself with organizing my office supplies. I have three packs of Post-It Notes (pink), four mechanical pencils, a stapler, and a desk calendar that they give out at the branches, the kind that folds into a triangle. I flip through the months. The July 1 holiday is on a Wednesday, the worst possible day. The August long weekend is nice and early, though, on the third, and Labour Day isn't until the seventh. Then it's on to Thanksgiving and Remembrance Day, before ending up at Christmas and Boxing Day on the last Friday and Saturday in December. I circle them all with a red marker. For some reason I have five of them. My future escapes from work are neatly mapped out.

Rick turns pages at a glacial pace. The twilight outside turns to darkness. Rick is still scrutinizing pages, red pen in hand. Just before nine o'clock he dumps the box back on my desk. "There are smudges in six of the books. The graph on page 7 is 0.0008 of an inch off square. The colour of the cover is half a shade lighter than our corporate brand. Get them fixed by tomorrow at seven thirty. I need to deliver them by eight," Rick says. "The production room is twenty-four hours." I'm pretty sure that when I go back to the sub-basement, I'll enter through a rusty, barbed-wire gate.

* * *

1988

My house has a small courtyard in the front, and a deck enclosed with an eight-foot-high fence in the back. There is no lawn to cut. I even have parking, immediately behind my deck, but of course I do not have a car. That would be about as useful as owning a chainsaw in the inner city. My car-and-a-half parking spot remains unclaimed, just beyond the (not barbed-wired nor rusty) eight-foot garden gate. Or at least it is supposed to be unclaimed. Every morning it's littered with misshapen pop cans, flattened in the middle with holes punched through the aluminum, with ash residue. This is really puzzling. I have a motion detector light at the entrance to the back gate, for which I am constantly replacing the light bulb that is either smashed or removed almost every night. Whatever's going on back there requires cover of darkness.

My street runs one-way south, as does the street beside it to the east. There is a No Right Turn sign where my street meets the street that runs perpendicular to the north, so it can only be approached westbound. Another puzzle. My block ends at Dundas Street East, right near a church that strangely has no pews nor church services.

The convenience store on the corner has bars on the window and emits a loud *beep* when you open the door. The cashier is in a cage behind bullet-proof glass. This is a store whose most valuable product on offer is scratch-and-win lottery tickets. It's a transitional neighbourhood, my real estate agent said, but gentrifying nicely. This is true only if you count the proliferation of hookers on the corner and drug deals going down in the alley as gentrified. Perhaps he meant the entrepreneurial commerce was expanding. Regardless, these are not the upscale hookers that work over at Jarvis and Carlton. No thigh-high, wet-look boots here. The most generous description is that we're in *Flashdance* territory: ripped sweatshirts and ripped jeans, except the rips are not at all deliberate.

Every day when I get home from work, I go up to my second-floor den and watch *The Young and the Restless*, which I tape in advance. The advantage of taping is that I can watch the entire hour of the program in twenty minutes, by fast-forwarding through the ads, and the long pauses when Nikki is on the phone with Mrs. Chancellor, or whomever is her nemesis du jour. I have watched *Y&R* for about ten years by now. It is a font of knowledge. Some lessons I take particularly to heart: it's sometimes hard to tell the difference between the good guys and the bad guys; always dress nicely at all times because you never know who you might run into; and there are only so many plot lines in life.

While I am catching up on the most recent events in Genoa City, the phone rings. I pause the tape, mid conversation between Victor and Paul, to pick it up. Dead air. Must be the duct cleaning company again. As I reach over to put the phone back in its cradle, I hear a voice. A familiar voice. "Where have you disappeared to now?" says The Cat.

"You know perfectly well where I am," I reply. "You phoned me."

"Dinner. Tuesday. Six. Bemelmans. Meet you there," he says. And hangs up.

Am I having dinner with a good guy or bad guy? This plot line has played out countless times. It will replay endlessly as long as I continue to pick up the phone. Or venture out anywhere in the greater Toronto area. What am I going to wear?

* * *

I notice, as I walk down the hall at work toward the bathroom, that Susan is sitting in her office, immersed in reading something. She must be preparing for the next briefing book. When I pass her doorway, she quickly slips a paperback into her top drawer, straightens the blotter on her desk, and sits up straight. She looks up with a sheepish look on her face. I don't really know Susan. She started about a month after me. I'm not even sure what her job is. Maybe I should learn more. I backtrack. Coffee break is in five minutes. "Hey Susan, want to grab a coffee?" She nods. "I'll get my wallet and meet you at the elevator," I say.

We head down to the cafeteria and get our drinks. "What do you think about Rick," I say.

"Well," says Susan, very carefully. "He cares about his job."

"I think he cares more about my job than his," I say. "At least he spends more time doing my job that his."

Susan snorts her coffee out her nose. "I thought I was the only one," she said. "This job is nothing like they explained it to me in the interviews. I spoke to ten people before I got the offer. It was like I was joining the Secret Service. They used a private investigator to do a background check. All I do is compile some numbers during the first week of the month and then I have nothing to do. I'm terrified Rick will find out and fire me. No, wait, maybe I hope Rick will fire me. This place is a nightmare."

Susan tells me Rick stores the background check documents in his credenza, and he keeps the key in his top-left desk drawer. "I made a copy of my report," she says. "It was horrifying. I think they interviewed my second-grade teacher and my hairdresser! All for this stupid, boring, useless job."

We chat about the briefing book paranoia and Rick's ridiculous rules. Meanwhile, I'm wondering when Rick will be out of the office next. I need to get my hands on that report. "It was Danielle Steel," Susan says. "The book I was reading. I have a whole stack of them in my drawer. I go through at least two a week. Borrow one if you like."

* * *

Rick bustles into the office on Monday and announces he must leave immediately for a meeting at one of the branch offices in Midtown. "I'm late," he says. "It's important. Please collect my messages while I'm gone," he says, looking at me. I guess if I'm a photocopy specialist, taking messages is firmly in my wheelhouse. However, it gives me a good excuse to skulk around his desk. I wait until the elevator has had time to get to down to the lobby, then riffle through his desk drawer to retrieve the key to his credenza. Susan says he keeps the employee files in the bottom drawer. I'm carrying a decoy file folder. If anyone walks by, I'll pretend I'm putting a file in instead of taking one out. I slide the drawer open and am scanning the folder labels when I see Dan from accounting briskly walking my way.

"Where's Rick?" he says. "Are you his assistant? When did he get an assistant? I need his expense reports today if he wants to get his cheque on Friday."

"Gone to Midtown Branch," I say. "I'll get them to you by end-of-day. Got some filing to do first." That was smooth. But how come Dan doesn't know who I am? He gives me the employees-per-branch stats every month. I hope he doesn't tell anyone about Rick's new assistant. Especially not Rick. I continue scanning the file folder tabs and then I see my name. It's a skinny file containing one document: a ten-page report from Britain Investigations. I lift it out, slip it inside my suit jacket, and close the file drawer. I slide the key into my pocket and head to the elevator, down to the copy centre. Office of the Chairman business. It should be ready in about two minutes, bound and everything.

By the time Rick gets back after lunch, the copy of the investigation report is sitting in my briefcase, the credenza is locked, and the key is back in his drawer. "Any messages?" he asks.

"No," I say. His expense cheque will not be showing up Friday. I hope it was a big one.

I don't open the report until I'm on the streetcar home. I feel like I'm a counter-spy spying on a spy. *Confidential. Top Secret*, it says at the top of the first page. It goes on to summarize my background. *The subject grew up in a strange town, near four nuclear reactors. Despite the fact everyone there worked as scientists for Atomic Energy of Canada, there is no evidence the subject ever took science after high school, and she never took physics after Grade 9. Which is to say, she never took physics at all. She failed math in Grade 11. Note, the fact she got eighty-five percent in Grade 11 math is because of summer school. She used to hitchhike home. Fifty miles. There is no evidence her mother knew about this.*

I wonder why they haven't mentioned spilling hydrochloric acid on my tights in chemistry? Five pages later, they've chronicled my life until I finished my undergraduate degree. Except they don't quite believe I did. *There is no evidence a degree was granted from Waterloo*, says the report. It goes on to editorialize: *It is not clear at all how the subject, with no known science or math background, got into Waterloo in the first place, let alone graduated.*

I guess U of T made a big mistake letting me into business school. I flip to the last two pages, which contain the results of my reference checks. "Strangely her references say the subject is an admired coworker who delivers excellent results. References also indicate the subject is proficient with working with men and is respectful of authority." Not surprising they got that last thing wrong. About two-thirds of everything in this report is factually incorrect. I got hired anyway. Unfortunately.

* * *

Bemelmans is on Bloor Street, just west of Bay. It kicks into high gear around eleven at night. On a Tuesday after work, I pass a sparse crowd of end-of-day beer drinkers as I make my way to the hostess podium. There are many empty tables, and no sign of The Cat. The go-go dancer cages are empty and the disco ball is resting for the night ahead, although I don't know anybody who would be hanging out here on a weeknight. I choose a spot where I can watch the entrance. According to the clock on the transfer machine at the Bay subway, I am here exactly on time.

I open my briefcase and take out a *Harvard Business Review*. I'm trying to figure out how to write an article about executive information systems. That would show Rick I can do more than babysit photocopiers. A few more people are coming in now, probably business-trip diners who want to see what all the fuss is about at the legendary resto-lounge. I have no idea what time it's getting to be, but I have drunk three glasses of water so far. I keep reading. When I look up next, I see the tables around me have emptied and filled up again. This dinner is clearly not happening. I shrug my raincoat on over my new red power suit. If a red power suit isn't seen, is it still a power suit? When the waitress walks to the back to pick up some plates, I saunter out of the restaurant. I'd get a new phone number except it's a hassle to change it and he'd find out the new one anyhow. I'll have to start screening my calls better. Everything is going to the machine from now on.

On Wednesday after work, I'm watching *Y&R* as usual when my doorbell rings. Hoping it's the dry-cleaning pickup, I grab an armful of shirts, skirts, and jackets and go downstairs to the front door. The Cat is on my doorstep. He just stands there, looking at me. "Just airing my dirty laundry," I say. My pilled black leggings peek out from under a bulky knee-length leopard-print sweater. The toenails of my bare feet show the vestiges of DayGlo-pink polish that was applied many weeks ago. My hair is end-of-day greasy. Mrs. Chancellor would not approve.

"It would be polite to ask me in," he says.

"It would be polite to keep a dinner date," I say.

"It would be polite to let me explain," he says.

"It would be polite to stop stalking me," I say.

Despite my better instincts, I deposit my clothing in a pile on the hall table, and motion for him to come into the living room. I forgot to pause my show. I can hear Nikki and Victor having a spirited discussion over spaghetti Bolognese and a bottle of Chianti at Gina's. This reminds me that I have nothing to eat in the house. But I do have wine. "Can I get you a glass of wine?" The Cat nods, but stays on the inside door mat, looking up at my ten-foot ceilings and the floating staircase that curves up from the basement to the third floor.

I plunk a bottle of wine and two glasses on the glass coffee table, light the fake log in the fireplace, and sit on the couch. The Cat unglues his feet from the mat, hangs his coat on the hooks by the door, and sits down beside me. "This is quite the place," he says. "You've moved up in the world. Not bad for an artsy girl." I pass him some wine. I will not say anything.

I walk over to the stereo and turn it on. Bob Dylan starts singing "Don't Think Twice, It's All Right" A fortunate coincidence. The Cat is looking at my décor. Persian carpets.

Sleek modern combined with 1930s shabby chic. I finally did get the orange chair reupholstered, in taupe velvet. There's a dish on the coffee table, filled with Murano glass candies in pastels. From a distance, they look like oval sweets wrapped in multi-coloured striped cellophane. The Cat picks one up and attempts to unwrap it. I stifle a snort of laughter and sit back down on the couch.

"Interesting Bob Dylan song," The Cat says. I maintain my silence. "Look," he says. "I got tied up and lost track of the time. Have a trial starting Friday. Can we do dinner after the trial? It should only take a week. I'll take you to Three Small Rooms if I win."

"What happens if you don't win? McDonalds?" I ask. Darn. So much for the silence thing.

"There's a lot going on in the real estate industry these days," he says. "You can see all the cranes for those condos by the lake. Business is booming." The Cat sips his wine. "I'm expected home by eight." I regain my silent composure. Bob Dylan has exited stage left. Now Bruce Cockburn is on deck, wondering where the lions are. "Haven't heard that in a while. Not since you ran off to Saskatoon," he says. "We should go to a club. See Morgan Davis. Go dancing. I never go dancing anymore." Right. As if that will ever happen. "How did I end up in the suburbs with a wife and kids?"

Um, bad choices? my inside voice replies. I drain my glass to prevent my mouth from kicking into gear. But it does because The Cat actually asks about my job, so I tell him about Rick-the-Dick, and the photocopying and the background report.

"You're smart," he says. "You've always been determined. Just get a new job. Everybody wants to hire women these days. I'd hire you but it would be too dangerous. I'd never get any work done." He thinks this is funny. "Anyhow, I must get on my way. The rush hour traffic should be clear by now. Call you Friday, once I know the trial schedule." He snags his Burberry off the hall coat hook, then grabs me around the waist and pulls me into the coat. He kisses me for ten minutes, then abruptly picks up his briefcase and heads out to his car. I watch as his Infinity pulls away from the curb. I wonder how long it would take to switch to an unlisted phone number.

* * *

It's a Friday at the end of the month. The briefing book went out this morning. Nothing to do until Monday, so I retrieve Thursday's paper from the garbage bin in the mail room. It is only slightly marred by coffee grounds. The business section is filled with employment want-ads. Almost as good as Saturday's paper. I scan the list. Librarian. No. Financial analyst. No. Rocket scientist. That would be a good one. If anyone says, "It's not rocket science," I can say, "Yes, it is. It is rocket science." Requires a Ph.D. in astrophysics. That's a no. But here's one. A consulting firm is looking for executive information system expertise. Only a handful of people even know what those are. And I'm one of them. Somebody might automate the bank's monthly briefing book, but it isn't going to be me. At least not as long as Rick-the-Dick is my boss. The Cat is right. I can get a new job. I can be a technology consultant.

15

Borrowing Watches

<u>1989</u>

In the interview, Kathy says consulting is not a career for people who need a place to keep their shoes. "We do all of our work at the client site," she says. "We only have enough office space for a fraction of our staff. If your bum is in one of our seats, you are an asset that's not making any money. You are a revenue-generating unit, and if you aren't doing that, your shoes have one foot out the door, along with all your other pairs of shoes that have no business being here in the first place." None of this deters me. There cannot possibly be a frying pan nor fire worse than the bank.

The Campbell, Talbot, and Associates office is on the third floor of a four-storey building on the northeast corner of Dundas and University. There's a Druxy's just off the entrance, well-known as the last resort for a semi-edible lunch. The elevator lobby is cramped and dingy, not at all like the opulence of 111 St. Clair nor the gilded, coffered ceiling of Commerce Court North. I will learn shortly that the name of the game in the consulting business is minimizing overhead. Fancy offices are the realm of our clients. The fancier the better, because their desire and ability to spend money is directly correlated with the opulence of their lobby.

When I show up on my first day, Kathy takes my picture with a Polaroid camera, and tacks it to a bulletin board in the room that triples as a mailroom, photocopy room, and coffee room. Since nobody's ever in the office, it's hard to know who actually works for CTA and what they look like. That's where the photo wall comes in. I will learn later that the photo wall also plays another important role. But not yet. My first day at the office turns out to be my last day in the office. I've been assigned to a project that starts tomorrow. At a bank. A bank that wants an executive information system.

* * *

The bank where I've been sent to work my consulting magic has a data centre on the southwest corner of Front and John Streets. There is no signage on the building, and the entry is through an airlock and turnstiles accessed via a magnetic card. It is top secret, to prevent terrorists or angry customers from blowing up the computers that hold all the bits and bytes that keep track of the bank's money. And sometimes even their customers' money. To get a magnetic card, I need to fill out a twenty-five-page security background questionnaire. I'm hoping that growing up in the company town for top-secret nuclear scientists will help, rather than hinder, this process. In my own defence, the spies had left long before we moved there. Maybe I should just supply a copy of the Britain report and save time answering the hundred questions, including everywhere I've lived in the past twenty years, and every address and phone number.

The reason I'm at the data centre is because the purpose of the executive information system is so the bank can figure out how much it costs to deliver electronic banking services. The bank has been offering electronic banking services for more than fifteen years, yet not until now did it decide it was necessary to know how much these things cost.

To improve customer service, it wants to encourage more people to use automated teller machines. To improve customer service, it wants to slash the number of physical branches. To improve customer service, it wants to reduce the number of physical tellers. I can see exactly how this will play out in the monthly briefing book of the other banks. This bank will have higher revenue per branch and higher profit per employee. Unless every bank does this, the competitive performance results will not be pretty. The thing is, though, if the bank wants to push more people to self-service, it needs to understand the full cost implications and the true cost-saving implications. So that's why I'm here. To do something nobody has successfully been able to do in the past fifteen years.

I'm camped out in a conference room that's been converted to a work space. There are some scarred wooden desks, some mainframe computer terminals (the ancient kind where the monitor and keyboard are all one piece), a barf-coloured industrial carpet, and a roommate.

Andreas is not from CTA. He is a freelance data scientist, and appears to be from somewhere in Eastern Europe, based on the number of consonants in his last name. He also appears to have only one outfit: a button-down white shirt, a moss-green V-neck cardigan with iron-on patches on the elbows that have been less than expertly ironed on, and dress pants with shiny knees. His cardigan smells like a pack-a-day Rothmans habit, and the nicotine stains on his first two fingers corroborate this. He has commandeered one of the terminals, and spends his days hunched over the keyboard, swearing in some Slavic language. Or at least I assume it's swearing, but he doesn't speak to me so I can't ask him.

We have our own printer, so I only need to leave the room to go to the bathroom or pick up lunch. Andreas leaves for lunch too, and also for a smoke break every hour. He clearly does not need to fill out a timesheet, because his lunch breaks last anywhere from two to three hours. I'm supposed to bill at least 7.5 hours a day. I'm not sure what happens if I don't, but I have no desire to find out. Andreas's job is to gather the raw data I need to develop a banking transaction costing algorithm. In the meantime, I'm studying up on the core banking systems, which were built in the late 1950s out of bailing wire and sealing wax. It's kind of like learning how hot dogs are made. I think after this I'll be keeping my money under my mattress.

The only good thing about being cooped up with Andreas is that the pointy part of our triangular room consists of floor-to-ceiling windows overlooking the construction of the SkyDome. It's supposed to be ready for the Blue Jays home opener on June 3. This does not look at all likely because a month out, they're still pouring concrete for the walls. But what do I know? Maybe it's less complicated than it looks to build a stadium with a retractable roof. And maybe banking systems are less complicated than they look too.

* * *

CTA's head office is in Montreal, and we have branches in Toronto and Québec City. We get memos every few weeks from head office in mangled English, talking about mandates and planification. Every three months we have a branch meeting after work, where we get updated on what's going on at the company. It's held at a hotel meeting room because we don't have any other place to do it. I've been at the bank for the past two months. If I end up in the wrong meeting room, I will have no way of knowing. I have no idea what any of my colleagues look like. I decide to stop into the office before the meeting to study the photo board. It is not a good idea. I will never be able to memorize all the faces and names in ten minutes.

When I get to the hotel, I find the room and choose a chair in what I hope is an inconspicuous location. I hate rooms full of strangers. I also hate rooms full of people I know. I also hate everything in between. It's like a class reunion for a school I didn't graduate from. Everybody is hugging and squealing and chatting about what's happened since the last meeting. Two women sit down in the row in front of me. They both look like real consultants, poised and knowledgeable. They probably have more glamorous assignments than me, like reverse engineering how to get the caramel into the Caramilk bar or solving world hunger using only a can of tuna and a box of Kraft Dinner. I busy myself writing entries for my timesheet in my notebook and making a to-do list for next week, but I can overhear their conversation.

"Went in to collect my telephone slips," the dark-haired woman says. "Have you seen the photo wall lately? Definitely some pictures have fallen off."

"Really?" the blond woman says. "Well, it is the end of the quarter. Who's been on the beach for a while? Tom? Helen?"

"I'm pretty sure they're still there, but it's always hard to tell. You know how they always reposition the other photos to fill the gaps. And they are never alphabetical. Pisses me off."

"Well, let's just keep our eyes peeled for who is and isn't here. Attendance is mandatory and all that."

Larry, the branch manager, calls the meeting to order. First round of business is anniversaries and new employees. Darn. Kathy didn't tell me new employees were on the agenda. Larry calls my name and asks me to stand up and say where I've come from and what assignment I'm working on.

"I came from Economical Bank, and before that Imperial Oil," I say. "This is my first consulting job. I don't think I'm allowed to tell you what I'm doing on my current project. I went through a background check and signed an NDA. I do not think Larry would like it if I had to kill all of you." Larry frowns and looks at his cheat notes. Nothing there to indicate I'm a smart ass. The women in front of me stifle laughter. The dark-haired one turns around and gives me the thumbs up. Larry drones on about utilizations statistics and profit margins and what's in the funnel.

"We have three months to make these numbers before our year-end," Larry says. He announces a hundred-dollar bonus for anybody who does something that helps with marketing or visibility, like giving a speech at a conference or writing an article that promotes our services. Larry ends the meeting with platitudes about us being "second to none" and having "a unique methodology" and "the best customers." I would have thought any customer is a good customer. But what do I know? I'm new to this consulting stuff. "Oh, and one more thing," says Larry. "Please remember we are not in the office supply business. Your clients should be your primary source for paper, pens, Post-It notes, and staplers."

There's a stampede to the refreshment table. The blond woman says, "Hope it's good today. If I'm doing this on my own time it should be worth a free dinner." There are lukewarm pizzas from Pizza Pizza, a case of Labatt Blue, and a few bottles of wine. "Wow," says the blond woman. "This is way better than last time!" I look at the congealed cheese and the labels on the wine. Surely the socializing part of the meeting is not included in the mandatory part. I casually saunter out of the room, hoping Kathy thinks I'm headed to the bathroom, and walk out of the hotel to the nearest streetcar stop. I am going to have that hundred dollars in my bank account before the end of the month. I'm going to buy a cordless telephone. A fancy pink one.

* * *

The Blue Jays home opener is three days away. Today, the first Friday in June, the activity outside the bank's conference room window involves a crane lowering gold-coloured sculptures that look like they are made from papier-mâché onto concrete platforms attached to the upper corner of the building. They are supposed to represent the sports fans that are soon to fill the new stadium.

This is so exciting that two dozen bank employees are crammed into my workspace, waving their coffee mugs and leaving doughnut crumbs on the carpet, enhancing the vomitous appearance of the décor. Andreas is ignoring all of this, muttering under his breath at a ream of output paper he has just pulled from the printer. At ground level, gardeners are scurrying around, rolling out turf on the median beside the main walkway, and installing flowers in planters. Maybe it will be ready for Monday after all.

Andreas shows up mid-morning after the weekend. Like every Monday, in addition to the tobacco, he smells like alcohol, and not just on his breath. It's oozing from his pores as if he bathed in it. Maybe it's an Eastern European ritual. He takes his usual spot at the terminal and pecks away at the keyboard. Less than an hour later, he looks at his watch, grabs the pack of cigarettes from the top of the desk, and heads for the elevator. I guess it's smoke-break time.

I continue my paper-based dissection of the innards of the deposit-management system, until I hear a roar outside. The gates of the stadium have opened and the crowd is streaming into the baseball game. The retractable roof is open, but I'm not high enough to be able to see in. Somehow, they pulled it off. "An inspiration to us all," Gord Martineau said on Citytv last night. "They gave it one hundred and ten percent! Go Jays!" I will not tell Gord that I saw the sausage being made and am not quite sure how the sculptures will continue to defy gravity. I'm also not quite sure how I'm going to get to the end of this project. I'll either die of old age, my photo on the board remaining a picture of Dorian Gray, or I will die of shame due to not being able to get it finished in time. And I can't do it without Andreas. There's a knock on the doorframe, and Jim, who works for the CIO, asks me if I've seen Andreas. "No," I say. "Haven't seen him since before lunch."

Jim sighs and rolls his eyes. "I guess that means I'm not getting the status report that was due Friday. Fred's not going to be happy. Hey, mind if I look out at the people heading to the home opener? The roof's open and everything! What will we do for amusement now that the dome is finished?" He walks to the window, stands right in the centre of the V and looks down at the Gate 13 entrance. "What the heck? Is that Andreas I just saw at the turnstile? You cannot mistake that ridiculous green cardigan." He almost trips as he runs out of the room. I'm still waiting for my stuff from Andreas too. I'm supposed to be working on the algorithm this week. The mockup of the EIS is due at the end of the month. It's like one of those recurring nightmares, where it's the day before the briefing book is due and all the photocopiers are out of order. And the elevators. And the subway. Everything points to me being toast.

* * *

When I call into the office to check, Vicky, the receptionist, tells me I have two telephone messages. I can hear her rifling through her vertical file for the pink slips. "The first one is from Kim Lewis, principal dancer at the National Ballet," she says. "Why would someone from the ballet call you?" Vicky is stuck in the office all day answering the phones but with little other human interaction. That's why she has to live vicariously through me and the other consultants. I haven't heard from Kim, my friend from when I lived on Bedford Road, for at least two years, and haven't seen her since I got back to town to go to business school. I thought she moved to England. This is really weird. She's not from the National Ballet, of course, that was just our running joke.

"You can have dibs on *Swan Lake*," she said, back when we were doing class with Joffrey. "I'm going to start in *La fille mal gardée*." Only she'd pronounced it "fill mal guard" instead of "fee mal gardez." On purpose. "That Karen Cain chick better watch out. We have pointe shoes and everything." Then we laughed and I'd reminded her how she used to fart when we did the entrechat quatres. It's her fault I'm afraid to go to a chiropractor in case I run into what's-his-name from Cowboys. Since I don't know what his name was, it would be kind of hard to deliberately avoid him.

"And the second one," Vicky says, "is from some guy called Morris. Like, who's called Morris? Like that cat in the ad? No last name. No company name. He left a number, though. Looks like it's the Bay Street exchange. Do you know who he is? He sounded kind of weird when he called. He didn't say anything at first, and I almost hung up before he finally asked to speak to you." The Cat! How does The Cat know where I work? Last time I talked to him I was at the bank. Oh. Wait. I know why. My article about EIS systems appeared in the business section of the paper yesterday. My hundred bucks is on its way.

* * *

Fred, the bank's CIO, has finally realized that Andreas is a liability. His legacy is an earth as scorched as the hastily applied turf from the home opener. He also left the remnants of a pack of Rothmans to add to the funeral pyre. On any given Monday morning, a single spark in that conference room would have immolated both of us via the vodka fumes. But the annihilation of Andreas, no matter how satisfying, causes me a world of butt hurt. The mockup of the EIS is still due. In two weeks. In a presentation to the office of the chairman. If this is not the definition of déjà vu, I don't know what is.

Jim knocks on the conference room door and hands me the key to Andreas's desk. "I had to get a locksmith in over the weekend," he says. "Andreas took off with the key." Excellent. Now I can riffle through the file drawers to see what I can salvage. I pull out a pile of folders and take them over to my desk to take a look. There are pages and pages of output, plus hand-scribbled notes in some language that is definitely not English. It takes the whole day to examine the contents of his desk. I find nothing.

I pull out the top drawer to put the folders back and notice that it is catching on something at the back. I bend down to see if I can figure out what's causing the problem. There's another file folder, wedged between the top and bottom drawer. I fish it out, tearing the cover in the process. Inside, there is a printout with a matrix of costs for the electronic bank transactions. It's dated a month ago. Andreas has been sitting on this for weeks. While pretending he was still working. I make several copies of the pages, just in case, then put a set in my briefcase to peruse on the way home.

* * *

The bank's executive board room is filled with various stakeholders talking about the Blue Jays and eating jelly doughnuts. The only person I recognize is Jim. I was supposed to review my presentation with him but he was out of town and we didn't have time. Jim calls the meeting to order and nods at me to start my spiel. I flick on the overhead projector and place my first transparency on the glass. I begin with the background about the project, the scope of what we examined, and the banking systems that were included.

Then I move to the parameters of the analysis and the key variables. Finally, the literal money shot. The transaction costs. According to Andreas, it costs 0.002 cents per deposit, 0.0004 cents per withdrawal, and 0.00006 cents per transfer. The men around the table look at this thoughtfully, making notes in their leather portfolios. The thing is, I know that the current fee for an online deposit is thirty cents, the fee for an online withdrawal is twenty cents, and the fee for an online transfer is twenty-five cents. The assembled executives can, of course, do the math. The automated teller machine is a licence to steal money. Jim nods approvingly. We have proven the value of automation beyond a doubt. But what we haven't proven is a reason to have a fancy executive information system. No need to track automated transactions very closely. The only thing the bank needs to do is continue to downgrade in-branch service to push customers to the instant teller. There won't be any follow-on work for this project. Kathy will not be happy.

16

Strategic Measures

<u>1990</u>

The Pickering Nuclear Generating Station sits on the north shore of Lake Ontario, just far enough to the east of Toronto to hopefully render it a mostly benign threat. There's a reason why the east side of a metropolis is always less desirable, and that reason is prevailing winds. Pollution, noxious substances, and nuclear meltdown byproducts typically move from west to east. The Pickering plant, which consists of four reactors, uses the CANDU version, which was designed in Chalk River, Ontario, at the first Atomic Energy of Canada facility. I grew up in the town that was established to house the scientists that invented it. That's why I know the CANDU is fortunately reasonably impervious to Chernobyl mishaps. Ontario Hydro, purveyor of energy in Ontario, has a bustling nuclear construction division that is in charge of maintaining the reactors and their infrastructure. Hydro's nuclear construction division is so certain of their continued exponential growth they have decided they need a technology strategic plan. And CTA was chosen to create it for them.

When I arrived back in the office after my stint at the bank, Reg, the account manager, informed me I was being assigned to the Hydro strat plan. Never mind that I've never done a real strat plan, just the pretend ones in business school several years ago, but I am very good at trotting out the abbreviation. Reg assured me Hydro would pay us handsomely for my learning curve. Our project office is at the Pickering plant site. "There's a strict dress code," Reg said. "You will be issued safety shoes, safety glasses, a hard hat, coveralls, and a dosimeter badge. No skirts or heeled shoes allowed." Wait. A dosimeter? I know all about dosimeters from my summer job at Chalk River.

A dosimeter badge is a square frame of plastic that holds a special type of photographic film that measures and records radiation exposure from gamma rays, X-rays, and beta particles. A dosimeter means business. I took a moment to sneak a peek at the photo board. It has been shuffled. Maybe I'm replacing one of the fallen from the Hydro project. Hopefully not due to catastrophic injury or death. Reg told me to be there on Monday morning at seven thirty, which is when the day shift starts at the plant. I thank Reg for the assignment, check my mail cubby for messages, and head home for the weekend. At least I have a couple of days to figure out how to get from downtown to Pickering without a car.

The first thing I learn on Monday morning is that when the commuter train says it will leave at 6:36 a.m., it does not mean it will leave at 6:37 a.m. After climbing three sets of worn concrete steps littered with gum and cigarette butts, via a stairwell that smelled like the hundreds of people before me who have puffed up the stairs, hauling their briefcases and lunch buckets, I finally got to the designated platform, only to see the west end of a train heading east on its way out of the station. I'm reluctant to walk down the stairs only to have to walk back up, but the electronic sign that would tell me when to expect the next train lives in the concourse. Down I go, to discover exactly how late I'm going to be. Very late. The next eastbound lakeshore train is at 7:36 a.m.

Fifty minutes later, I disembark at the Pickering GO station. I run to catch the local bus that I hope will take me down to the plant gate. From there, it's a fifteen-minute hoof on a muddy path to the enclave of construction trailers that serves as our project office. Reg was right. No high heels need apply.

The trailers are no-nonsense rectangles: open-tread metal steps to a steel door that is flanked by two small windows. I turn the doorknob to my assigned trailer, entering a space crammed with wooden trestle tables and the kind of folding plastic chairs that live in church basements everywhere, beloved for their ability to be stowed away compactly and deplored for their inability to sustain a comfortable sitting position for longer than thirty seconds. This, apparently, will be my ergonomic work space for the duration.

Tim, who has been on the project for a few weeks, looks up when I enter. "We had a pool," he says. "How late will she be? I think I won. So far, though, you are only in the top five of tardiness. It took Reg until after lunch time when he first showed up. He tried to pretend he planned it that way. Except he had promised to take me for lunch."

Tim gets up from his spot at the big table in the middle of the room to show me around. It does not take long. What I see is pretty much what I get. Pretty much nothing. Not even a bathroom. Tim tells me the trailer next door has a kettle and microwave that we can use. He's not quite sure where the heat is going to come from in the winter, but we have a month or two to figure that out. "The bathroom trailer is over by the fence so we don't have to smell it too much," Tim says. "The lunch truck comes at eleven forty-five. Make sure you get in line right away or you'll be stuck with a mystery-meat sandwich. The coffee is passable, though." Great. The only thing I don't want is the only thing worth having.

I settle in to read a precariously stacked pile of background documents and previous deliverables. I'm neck deep in trying to comprehend the incomprehensible, when there's a knock on the door. A welcoming committee, perhaps. But instead of warm greetings, there are three Hydro guys on the front step, one wearing a white hard hat and two wearing yellow ones.

The white hat waves a pink piece of paper. "Requisition to install window blinds," he says, as they tromp into the trailer and survey the domain. I guess this is so we don't get distracted by the random rays of sun that might make it through the ten-by-fifteen-inch windows on three sides of the trailer. I leave them to their task, but in the cramped quarters, I can't help noticing what's going on. The foreman, who turns out to be the guy in the white hat, instructs one of the yellow-hat guys to measure the window and record the measurements. The other guy must be an apprentice because his job appears to be watching the measuring. "Hey, Tim," I say, "are there blinds in the other trailers?" Tim nods emphatically.

The measuring takes about an hour. Then the coffee-break truck arrives, honking louder than the geese that gather between the trailers and the lakeshore. "Union coffee time," says the foreman. "Then we'll go to the supply depot and get the blinds." They come back an hour later. One of the yellow-hat guys carries several boxes of vinyl venetian blinds that look exactly like the ones I have on my bathroom windows at home. I installed them myself in about ten minutes. The apprentice's job is to take the blinds out of the boxes and verify that all the hardware is there, while his two supervisors look on, watching for wayward screws, I assume. I know that's important because I lost one down my heating vent. Luckily, there were a few extra in the package.

Then, the reason for the two-man crew becomes apparent. Each guy takes one side of the window, and screws in the brackets that hold the blind. The sound of the lunch truck's horn blasts through the tin walls of the trailer, signalling the beginning of the union lunch break. My window-covering crew lays down their tools, and goes off to buy their dubious sandwiches, which they take over to the picnic tables that sit between the office trailers.

Precisely forty-five minutes later, it's finally time to tackle the actual hanging of the blinds. The apprentice is allowed to take the lead in this task, under the anxious gaze of the foreman and the senior blind installer, but it gets completed without serious incident. The blinds go up and down and swivel appropriately when they turn the plastic wand-like thing. They spend a few minutes admiring their work before leaving for the day, at three thirty sharp.

I figured that would be the end of Operation Sun Deflection, but I was wrong. Apparently, nuclear construction guys are always mindful of quality, since quality is an extremely important preoccupation when constructing and repairing nuclear things. The next morning, a green-hatted quality-control inspector arrives. He takes out a level, checks each blind, and records his findings in a big red binder. "Sign this, please," he says, passing me a three-part quality-report form. I sign and he hands me the pink copy, then files the yellow copy in his red binder. I am not quite sure what I'm supposed to do with the pink copy. Although I don't know it yet, I have just learned more than I will ever glean from the stack of reports on my desk. I have just been a frontline witness to the finer points of nuclear construction.

* * *

My work wardrobe has devolved into t-shirts, hoodies, and jeans, and by the end of the day, everything is spattered with mud from trips to the food truck, bathroom trailer, and safety office. I'm living the dream of the glamorous management-consulting career. Monday morning is always status meeting day in the main trailer. I've finished my two-week orientation, so now I get to find out what my main project task will be.

Reg plunks a box of doughnuts on the conference table in front of the eight of us waiting for the meeting to begin. Jen, the project coordinator who takes the minutes and minds the office supplies, taps her pen on her coffee mug to call us to attention. "First," says Reg, "thank you all for your work so far. The client is very happy. But now, we are entering another phase in the project and we'll all have to shift our tasks to define what needs to be done to implement the strat plan. We do not want to be accused of generating shelfware for a crown corporation."

Everybody nods knowingly. Shelfware is consulting reports for which the client has paid tens of thousands of dollars but which are sidelined to a shelf, with the expensive recommendations destined to go nowhere. Jen goes around the table, soliciting status updates.

"Finished the existing systems inventory."

"Validated the data model."

"The schematics of the network are complete."

Then it's my turn. "The blinds have been installed in my trailer." Reg does not think this is funny, but Jen guffaws as she dutifully records this in her notebook. Reg begins doling out our weekly marching orders:

"Research the EDM options."

"Drill down on the process maps. Physical level, please."

"Stress-test the VPN."

"Bombard the security system."

"Work the data model." Reg says this looking directly at me. He motions to Jen, who hands me a three-inch binder. I have no idea what working the data model means. I open the binder, which holds at least a hundred pages, and flip through it.

"Um, Reg," I say, "are there particular parts you think need working?"

"Many," he says. "But start with the entity 'Work Event.' That's all for today. See you here next week. Same bat time, same bat trailer." He is the only one who laughs at his joke. He picks up his cashmere coat and heads out the door. We hear his Jaguar rev up and spin its tires in the mud before tearing off up the hill to the highway. Not surprisingly, Reg prefers the comfort of his corner windows back at the office to the trailer wasteland, but he has to show up once a week to be able to bill the exorbitant project management overhead fee. At least he didn't take the uneaten doughnuts.

This is what I know about my new assignment. A data model maps out all of the bits that are essential inputs to the management information systems we are investigating. It documents the data elements and the stuff about them that need to be collected and stored to make it possible to generate the reports and analysis necessary to make management decisions.

The data model has to be complete and detailed, so nothing is less specific than it should be and nothing crucial is left out. Necessary and sufficient is the data model mantra. The visual representation of the data model is a chart containing boxes and lines. Each box has a name and is connected to other boxes with lines that either end in a chicken foot or don't end in a chicken foot. If there's a chicken foot, it means many. One employee can work on many jobs. One job can have many locations. One location can have many jobs. The diagram I'm looking at has a box sitting in the middle, with all four sides littered in chicken feet. A massive free-range hen party.

The place where all the chickens come home to roost is called "Work Event." Contrary to Kathy's warning that not everyone is suited to the life of a consultant, I'm finding it fits me perfectly. On the plus side, there are problems to solve and nobody tells me how I should go about solving them. On the minus side, there are problems to solve and nobody tells me how to go about solving them. I peruse the data model binder more closely on the train home. A Work Event is apparently a thing completed as part of a nuclear construction project. It has a beginning, middle, and end. The beginning is when it starts and it ends with a quality check. The middle is the middle. I flip forward and backward, but cannot find any details about the middle. I'm guessing this is what Reg means by working the data model. Figure out what happens in the middle. He wants me to paint a picture of the contents of a black hole. In Technicolor.

* * *

The slate roof on my house has been doing its job for more than a hundred years. One thing it excels at is shedding snow. My winter mornings are not complete without a *rumble* and *whoosh* as the steep pitch and slippery shingles join forces to divest themselves of their load, and this morning is no exception. I'll need to go down and shovel the mound that has landed on my front steps, if only to unearth my newspaper. But it's the weekend, so I can do it at my leisure. Lazing in bed by myself holds no appeal, though. I'm two storeys up from a cup of tea that will not make its way here on its own. I hear the neighbour that's attached to my left side out shovelling already. Wonderful. Leisure is now officially out of the question. I throw on some jeans and a tattered sweatshirt, wind my way down to the kitchen, and put the kettle on. Surely snow removal can wait for another ten minutes.

After I've finished sipping my Earl Grey, I pull on my boots and mitts and open the front door. Mike, my neighbour, has finished dismantling his portion of the avalanche. "Um," he says. "Are you missing a cat?"

"No," I say. "I don't have a cat." What's with the cat thing? Why does everybody want me to have a cat or think I must have a house full of cats? Do I look that pathetically single?

"Oh," he says. "I found a dead one under the roof snow. Must be someone else's." At least it wasn't under my pile. I start shovelling, hoping the cat was not travelling with a friend. I get down to the bottom without encountering any bodies. I shake the snow off my *Globe and Mail.* Maybe Mike and I should put up a warning sign. Next time it might be the paper boy.

17

Workin' It

<u>1991</u>

Fred, the new branch manager, taps the microphone with his finger. "Is this thing on?" he says, unleashing a burst of feedback. This does not stop him from continuing to mess with the sound system, until the hotel's AV tech runs up to help adjust it. Fred holds up his hands in mock surrender while the mic gets fixed. "Thank you for a wonderful year," he says. "Give yourselves a round of applause!"

There's a tepid response because we are too busy demolishing our catered dinner of fancy food. Lobster tails, risotto, and spinach salad with disks of fried goat cheese. Undoubtably, there will be profiteroles for dessert. I'm sitting at one of eight round tables that seats ten, with nine other consultants from the Pickering project. Tim's sitting to my left. He leans over and whispers, "I heard from Stu that Fred's got big plans. Stu also says many smiling faces are going to tumble off the photo wall next week." I move my risotto delicately onto my fork with my knife and am raising it to my mouth when Tim jostles my elbow and adds, "Don't be buying that yacht you have your eye on just yet. Apparently, our bonuses are going to be more in rubber duckie territory." My risotto lands in my lap, leaving a blotch of grease on the skirt of my favourite suit. Fred continues droning on about EBITDA and profit contribution, as I dunk my napkin in the dregs of my water glass and dab at the food in my lap.

Fred shifts his overhead slide to next year's growth projections. His graph shows a revenue line that chugs along at about $100 million for the first three months, then rises dramatically for the following three quarters. "Hockey stick growth," snorts Tim. "We learned about that in B-school but I never thought I'd see one in real life." I'm still trying to rescue my skirt by emptying my glass of water directly on the offending stain. Meanwhile, Fred starts explaining his visual.

"In order to achieve the growth we want and the profit we need, we will have to do more with less. We need to right-size, normalize, and optimize. We need to actualize our backlog, mobilize our sales efforts, and realize our deliverables. Give yourselves another round of applause!"

Tim starts banging his dessert spoon on his wine glass. Soon, the whole room sounds like a bride and groom should be locking lips. "See?" he says. "Check the board next week. Bloodbath guaranteed."

Figuring out which photos are gone has turned into a subversive project. On the third Monday of the month, somebody volunteers to take a tour of the mailroom and makes a list of the names on the photo board. Then, on the fourth Tuesday, the designated sleuth returns, under cover of end-of-day, and makes another list, thus revealing the consultants who have been torched this month. We pass the news around like cryptographers, spreading news of fallen comrades using only initials. "KD, HM, IB, RIP." Consultants who walk out the door, voluntarily or not, leave with the entire contents of their head. Fred believes our intellectual property lives inside the methodology binder. Fred apparently also believes in unicorns and free lunches.

Fred moves to the next agenda item. The annual awards. There are trophies and envelopes lined up on a table at the front of the room. First, he announces that Jane has won best team player, for having moved through twelve different projects in her first eight months. "Right," I whisper to Tim. "Best team player means the person nobody wants on their project, so that's why she's been punted so often her butt has dents in it." Jane receives an individual plaque, plus temporary custody of the group plaque that now bears her name. Nobody has ever heard of the other names, since the recipients never lasted more than a year before their photos hit the wastebasket.

Next, Reg is summoned to receive the sales prize. Fred gives him a triangular plexiglass trophy, a fat envelope, and what looks like a set of car keys. "Reg would sell his grandmother's false teeth," Tim says. "Even if she didn't have false teeth. No, wait, scratch that. Especially if she didn't have false teeth." Then it's time for the biggest award of the night. Outstanding contributor. I am still preoccupied with trying to salvage the carnage on my skirt, succeeding only in making it bigger and more obvious. Tim elbows me in the ribs, causing his half-used pat of butter to fly off his side-plate into my lap. Butter side down. "You!" Tim says. "Fred's calling you!" Sure enough, Fred is pointing at my table. I stand up, butter still clinging to my lap, and make my way to the front of the room.

Fred shakes my hand and says loudly to the room at large, "I guess you liked the food so much you decided to take it home!" He pauses for laughter, then reverts to his branch manager voice, and says, "I've asked Reg to say a few words." I stand beside Reg as he itemizes the accomplishments that earned me the award. I solved the most important problem facing the Hydro's Nuclear Construction department. A problem, if left unsolved, would prevent implementing the strat plan. A problem, if left unsolved, would result in all of the follow-on projects being cancelled. A problem, if left unsolved, would cause him to start the year six months behind in his quota. Actually, Reg did not mention that part. But we all know it's true. I accept Fred's congratulations as he hands me the tangible mementoes of the award, glad to have something to hold in front of my skirt as I reclaim my seat.

"Open them! Open them!" says Tim. My prize turns out to be a gold Cross pen and pencil set engraved with my name and a crisp $100 bill. "Well, you know," says Tim, "Reg always tells us not to confuse selling with delivery. At least the pen has your name on it so nobody can steal it. But on second thought, just to be safe, make sure you never show it to him." There is no need for Tim to point out that if it wasn't for us and the other consultants, nothing would get delivered so nothing could get billed so Fred's hockey stick would never materialize.

* * *

Four Months Earlier

The construction foremen are gathered in the trailer that serves as the conference room, fresh from their smoke break. The lingering aroma of Export A unfiltereds hangs around the room, as delightful as a smouldering pile of tires in a junkyard. I stand up and throw a piece of puke-green vinyl floor tile on the table. This succeeds in getting them to stop talking about the hockey pool and look in my direction. My hoodie, which I got at Value Village, says *Go Leafs Go!* on the front, and my coffee mug, which holds only water, says *Go Jays Go!* When in Pickering, do as Pickering does.

"Are we quality checking flooring today? Is that what this meeting is about?" says Bruce, the electrical foreman. "I was just told to show up, but flooring is not my department." He picks up his hardhat and starts toward the door.

"You are here," I say, "because Dave told you to be here. And I'm here because Dave is paying me to be here. Otherwise, there are many other places I would rather be, including places where I don't need to put my coat on to visit the bathroom. The importance of this meeting will become clear, but for now, all you need to know is that's a piece of floor. Whoever's talking gets to hold it. It's called having the floor." This gets a chuckle from everyone except Bruce. I hand the scrap of tile to Jim, the infrastructure foreman. Somehow, this intrigues Bruce and he sits back down, waiting to see how this is going to play out. "Jim," I say, "remember installing the blinds in my trailer? How many times would you say you've installed that kind of blind?" Jim reaches into the breast pocket of his coveralls, pulls out a notebook, retrieves the yellow nub of a pencil from behind his ear, and starts writing. We wait while he adds, subtracts, multiplies and divides.

"I reckon, over the past two years, about two hundred and thirty-six," says Jim.

"Great," I say. "And how long did it take you to do each one, on average?"

"Well, we never know exactly how long it will take. There could be so many things that make it different. That's why we need to allow lots of buffer in the job and keep extra staff on standby just in case."

My inside voice is incredulous, but I keep my outside voice calmly neutral. I grab a black marker and position myself in front of the flipchart. "Jim has a good point," I say. "Many things can happen that make one job different from another. Tell me what those might be." As they shout out items, I write them on the chart paper: the weather, the size of the window, the configuration of the room, the height of the building, the direction it's pointing, the type of roof, the number of light fixtures, the number of doors, the time of year. "What if," I say, "you could know about these variables in advance of the job?" Jim, Bruce, and the other guys around the table look at me with pity. I do not have a white hard hat, only a yellow one.

Bruce explains, "We work in nuclear construction. We cannot predict when our jobs come up. There's science going on here, you know. What if we need to install a new construction trailer tomorrow and we only find out at end-of-day today? How can we possibly plan in advance for the steps and the railings and the electrical hookup and the blinds and the flooring that we'll need?"

I take a moment to digest what Bruce has said. Then, I ask them to think about the things that are always needed when setting up a new construction trailer and the things that are sometimes needed. "Let's call 'setting up new construction trailer' a 'Work Event.' It has a beginning, middle, and end. Let's assume we're at the beginning. We've gotten the work order. What happens next?" I draw a line down the middle of the flip chart paper and label one side *Always* and the other side *Sometimes*.

"Wait," says Jim. "Can you define 'always'?"

After a few weeks of regular meetings with the foremen, they're starting to get in the Work Event groove. I feel like Henry Higgins teaching Eliza Dolittle proper English, only in this case I am teaching them to see the world without the distortion of safety glasses. At the next Monday gathering, Bruce sets a box of Timbits in the centre of the table. "I won the hockey pool," he says. "Timbits on me for the rest of the month."

"Speaking of pools," I say, "it's time to pony up for the lottery pool." I'm the custodian of our exclusive Work Event get-rich plan. So far, it's not panning out.

"You know how I told you that some trailers don't need steps?" says Jim. "That's not correct. They only end up without steps if the customer didn't ask for steps. Then what happens is we go back a week later and install the steps because they need steps to get in the door. They're all pretty mad too."

"You know how I told you that fluorescent light fixtures take longer to install than regular light bulbs?" says John. "That's not true. As long as the wiring has been finished, a fixture is a fixture. We usually send two guys for the fluorescents because they are longer, but I'm told the second guy just hands the other guy the light bulb. I never would have known this if I hadn't learned to ask the questions."

"You know how I told you we have to wait two days after the subfloor is installed before we can put the tile down?" says Peter. "That's not right. You only have to do that if you are at an unheated work site, but since 1985 all of our sites are heated with portable propane heaters."

I walk them through the data model as it now stands. A Work Event has many work streams. Each work stream has many tasks. Each task has many steps. Each step has a standard time estimate. If you add up the time estimates for each step in a task, add the tasks together, then add the work streams together, you get the total estimate for the Work Event. Everybody nods in agreement. "Okay," I say, "looks like we're ready to test this out on the next project."

"We're building a Quonset hut near reactor two," says Jim. "It'll use all of the trades. That can be our proof-of-concept." I tell Jim to gather together whoever he needs to map out and document the work streams and tasks, and create the estimates. "Great," he says. "Can you do tomorrow morning?" I wasn't exactly planning on getting myself this deep into the entrails of the data model, but I tell Jim I'll be there and I volunteer to take notes. Two birds, one stone. I'll need to document the results from end-to-end anyhow. And I've seen Jim's writing. He should have been a doctor.

Miraculously, the Quonset hut rises on time, but even more miraculously, under budget. In the debrief meeting, which is also our final taskforce meeting, Jim says this has never happened before. "I think the trick is," he says, "everybody knows exactly what their part of the job is and knows they have done it before. They just get right to it, instead of having to figure stuff out and go looking for components that aren't on the site." The final deliverable for my Work Event Project is a binder containing a hundred-page handbook that documents the standard tasks we've itemized so far. Jim, Bruce, and the rest of the foremen will add to it as new tasks are uncovered. I list my entire taskforce as co-authors. Reg is not happy with this move.

"What do you mean the client gets some of the credit? That's a slippery slope! Pretty soon they'll think they can do it all themselves, then it's bye-bye revenue and bye-bye bonus!" he yells through the phone. I hang up on him and send the original off to the copy centre to create thirty copies of the handbook, one for every foreman and deputy foreman. What Reg fails to get is that now they all own the deliverable. No shelfware here. My work is done. I am starting a new project on Monday, at Hydro head office in the city. No more bathroom trailer. No more train. No more Spam sandwiches.

18

Herding Documents

<u>1992</u>

When the calendar snaps sharply over to a new fiscal year, everything starts fresher than a free-range organic egg. The previous year's accomplishments are instant ancient history, interesting only to those who cling to the hope that the past will predict the future. Last year's salesman of the year could become this year's "Brian who?" Last year's consultant of the year could spend this year in the middle of the pack, inches away from photo-board hara-kiri.

Today, I start my new project, a Hydro follow-on deal Reg closed just before year-end. Our job is to create and test a prototype electronic document management system to process and store all the engineering specifications and related correspondence required for the retubing of the Bruce Nuclear Generating Station. Their CANDU reactors have a bunch of fuel channels that pass through a large cylindrical vessel called a calandria, which contains heavy water to cool the fuel rods. An important part of the reactor is the pressure tubes that hold the coolant. Turns out, they are getting worn out but they weren't designed to be replaced. Unless they are fixed, a billion dollars' worth of electricity generation hardware will be headed for the junk heap. There's also another problem. No equipment exists to complete this delicate and dexterous repair task.

"You're a librarian, right?" Reg said when he informed me that I was going to run the new project. "I told the client you were an electronic document management expert and that you're the perfect person to design the prototype." There was no point in arguing about the impossibility of something that Reg had already sold. I'll just have to figure it out.

After a leisurely walk from my house, which is a welcome change from the three-part two-hour transit trip to Pickering, I arrive at a curved glass building at the corner of College and University and take the elevator to the sixth floor. My new project office is an open-concept enclave about as far away from the windows as it could possibly be. Ben and Gavin, my project team, are already messing about with a Unix server when I arrive. They are busy "pinging" each other's desktop workstations and creating nicknames for the devices. "Okay," says Ben. "The server will be R2D2. I'll be Han Solo and you'll be Darth Vader." He says this with a straight face, and Gavin nods gravely as he makes notes in the project logbook. No doubt there is a Unix naming protocol that requires strict adherence to pop culture.

I clear a spot on one of the ledges that serves as desk space, and dump my jacket on the floor in the corner, which is the only place to put it. Ian, the Hydro lead for the document management project, leans over the cubicle partition. He points to a woman standing in our doorway. "This is Brenda," he says. "I've assigned her to your project team. See you at the requirements meeting this afternoon." Brenda looks like she dropped out of beauty school to form a punk band. Her short, platinum hair has been coaxed into spiky clumps. I have not seen that shade of blue eyeshadow since 1972, so I assume she's being ironic. Her frilly white blouse is tucked into a plaid mini-skirt that was probably her high school uniform ten years ago. I smile and tell her to make herself at home. "I'll be back in a minute," I say. "Maybe go to the supply cupboard and get what you need for your desk in the meantime." I head to a vacant cube at the other end of the hallway to call the office. "Reg," I hiss into the phone. "Who the hell is Brenda?" As I suspected, Reg knows exactly who Brenda is.

"You should be proud, as a woman, to have Brenda seconded to your project team. She's part of an affirmative action initiative to get more women into management. You are going to help her learn how to run projects."

"Um, Reg," I say. "Doesn't that mean we lose the opportunity to place another one of our own consultants?"

"Okay. Here's the thing. We have to take Brenda or you can't have both Ben and Gavin. Make sure you keep her happy. She'll be reporting back to Ian every week on her progress. And by the way, she's his niece."

Maybe I can make Brenda our official scribe and project administrator. Maybe wishes are horses. Maybe horses are unicorns.

* * *

Hydro has contracted several engineering firms to design and build the various devices needed to complete the retubing. This means there will be lots of documents being sent back and forth to be reviewed, approved, revised, reapproved, and then kept for posterity in case something goes wrong with the repair process, and given the slightest chance, something could go terribly wrong. They have chosen software called Interleaf to manage the engineering documents and their workflow. It only runs on Unix. Apparently, engineers like Unix because it's good at running specialized engineering stuff like CAD/CAM. I dearly hope it's also good at processing words and pages.

Before we can start configuring the prototype, we need to know exactly what kinds of documents it is going to manage and all the details about them. We are going to find this out via a series of meetings with the people who will be creating, revising, reviewing, and approving them. The first meeting is today, and the group is assembled around the conference room table.

"Is this the Willow Room? Am I in the right place for the meeting?"

"Are we going to end by three thirty? I come in at seven thirty and I leave at three thirty."

"Are those doughnuts for us? Can someone pass me a chocolate dip?"

"Anyone need a coffee? I'm going to go across the street."

"We can't start without Bob. Has anyone seen Bob? Jim, go and find Bob."

Ian sticks his first and second fingers in his mouth. The shrill whistle gets everyone's attention. Fifteen minutes gone so far. I review the agenda and objectives for the meeting. "Ian," I say, "why don't we make Brenda the scribe? We'll need to capture a lot of detail." Ian pulls a tape recorder out of his briefcase and puts it on the table beside the doughnuts.

Ian says, "Brenda will learn better by observing. Besides, we can send the recording down to the typing pool to transcribe it. We won't miss a thing." He has a point. That might actually be a good idea. At least I won't have to rely on Brenda. We proceed to explore types of documents and their relative importance, which thankfully unearths a lot of key points about what we'll need to cover in the prototype. There will be schematic diagrams as large as eight square feet. There will be pencil sketches on onion-skin paper. There will be notations on the back of cigarette packages.

"Wait," I say. "Cigarette packages?"

"Of course," says Ian. "What if you're out in the field and have nothing to write on? Everybody has a pack of cigarettes in his pocket."

"Couldn't we just give everyone a notebook?" I ask.

"I'm not sure the union would allow that. Extra gear to carry," says Ian. "I'll check."

The next day I call down to the typing pool to check on the progress of the transcription. They are supposed to be able to turn things around within twenty-four hours and I can't do anything until I get the meeting notes. "Everything is going well," says Molly, the head typist. "The tape is nice and clear, and I have two shifts on it." But as the week wears on, there is still no sign of the notes. I call again to ask if I can get at least a portion of the transcript to work from in the interim, and send Brenda down to collect the first part of the notes. She comes back with a thick interoffice envelop. I unwind the closure and lift out about seventy-five neatly typed pages. I sit down to see what I've got.

"Is this the Willow Room? Am I in the right place for the meeting?"

"Are we going to end by three thirty? I come in at seven thirty and I leave at three thirty."

"Are those doughnuts for us? Can someone pass me a chocolate dip?"

"Anyone need a coffee? I'm going to go across the street."

"We can't start without Bob. Has anyone seen Bob? Jim, go and find Bob."

(Sound of whistle).

I flip through the stack. The real stuff starts on page fifteen, but even then, they've transcribed every dropped pencil, coffee refill, and cough. Brenda couldn't possibly be worse than this. I think Ian's tape recorder will mysteriously disappear.

* * *

Gavin is waving the Arts section of the weekend newspaper. "It's our Brenda!" he says. There's a photo of the cast of a play that's running at the Tarragon Theatre. Sure enough, Brenda is front and centre. "How come she never told us she writes plays?"

"Gavin, she barely says anything. I don't think she'd ever tell us about something like this." But it gives me an idea. Maybe her talents aren't all hidden.

Gavin sees Brenda coming through the cubicle doorway and starts waving the paper again. "Brenda! We didn't know you were famous!" Brenda blushes and swats the paper out of his hands.

"Brenda," I say, "now that we have the requirements done, we're moving on to construct the prototype, but we'll also need a script for the demonstration that will show how the engineers will use the system in their day-to-day activities. Is that something you could do?" Brenda perks up and says she'd be glad to write the demo script. This is a big relief. I'm finally able to give her a real task instead of make-work ones.

I'm feeling very positive as I leave for the day. This gig may be a success after all. I'm preoccupied with my visions of triumph, so I don't immediately hear my name being called, but eventually I notice someone is trying to get my attention. It's Sam, The Cat's best man. He's standing about five feet in front of me, and I'm stuck in the wide-open terrace in front of the Hydro building. Nowhere convenient to hide. "I thought that was you," says Sam. "Are you working here now?"

"Not exactly," I say. No way I'm going to divulge anything specific to Sam. I know precisely where the information will end up.

"Want to grab a drink? Catch up on life since Imperial Oil?" Sam says.

"Can't today," I say. Drat. Why did I say not today? That implies I might be willing to do it another day.

"I'm up on the fifth floor," says Sam. "I'm sure I'll run into you again. Maybe next time."

"That's my streetcar," I say, and run to catch the College car that's just pulled up to the corner. I doubt I'm safe from the inevitable. It will only be a matter of time before The Cat shows up.

* * *

There is hardly enough room for all of us at the office, but Fred has called an emergency meeting, so it's standing room only. I see Tim come in at the last minute, and he squeezes in beside me just outside the doorway to the boardroom. He always knows what's going on. "Tim, what's going on?" I say. He shakes his head and mouths, *No idea*. Fred starts to talk.

"This will be in the press tomorrow, so I wanted to make sure you all know in advance. CTA has been sold to a division of Nynex, headquartered in New Jersey. All of our Canadian offices are included in the sale. An orderly transition will take place over the coming months. Business as usual until then and likely after. We are a going concern. Carry on and keep up the billable hours! My purchase transition bonus depends on it." Of course, he doesn't even say this in jest. He fully intends to protect his spoils against spoilage. We shuffle out of the office and Tim, Rick, Gavin, and I end up at the Fox and Firkin on Bay Street for a debrief.

"I told you that hockey stick was hinky," says Tim. "Do you think we'll lose our jobs?"

"I don't know," I say. "But I have no plans to leave unless somebody pays me to leave. Plus, I'm still knee-deep on the Hydro project. We have months more work just to get to the prototype, then there'll be configuration and implementation and training. I figure I'll be there for another year at least." Tim thinks his predicted bloodbath will happen in the next couple of weeks. We sit silently with our draft beer, contemplating our futures or lack thereof.

When I get to the project office on Friday, Gavin is waving the newspaper again. "Did you see this? Hydro just announced it has the largest surplus capacity of electricity in its history. Like, since 1906 when it was founded. The Bruce retube is being cancelled. I guess we don't want the price of electricity to go down. That would be bad for everyone. Well, maybe not everyone, just the people who work for Hydro." I scan the article, and it looks like Gavin is right. All the same, I'm not going to assume anything until I hear from Ian. Right on cue, he appears at the cubicle doorway.

"Special project meeting in an hour in the Willow Room," he says. "Just the project managers." But when I arrive, it's not just Ian, me, and the engineering managers in the room. There are all sorts of other people from the executive floor I've only met in passing. A grey-haired guy is getting ready to speak, while his assistant hands out press releases. He tells us pretty much what was in the paper. Too much power. Bruce A can be shut down and mothballed until it's needed. There will be no retubing, and hence, no need for specialized retubing equipment or complicated document workflow. The meeting is over in ten minutes, and Ian quickly scurries off somewhere. I guess I should call Reg, but why bother? He probably knew about this last week. Or more likely, a month ago. There's no point hanging around here, twiddling my fingers until further instructions. I grab my stuff and head home.

I sit on the couch and spend some time reviewing the original project proposal documents to see if there is any provision for cancellation. None is in evidence. I might as well watch my *Y&R* tape. As usual, I fast-forward through the commercials, I flip through takeout menus, dividing my attention between the drama of life in Genoa City and the events unfolding at work over the past few days. Hah! Work events! If that's not irony I don't know what is. I'm deciding between pizza and Chinese when my phone rings. I know exactly who is on the other end even before I pick it up. "Why are you hiding from me?" says The Cat. "Sam says you are looking good, by the way." I slam the receiver down and disconnect the phone jack from the wall. Believe me, Victor and Nicki, your soap-opera life has nothing on mine.

19

Sold Out

<u>1992</u>

More people must have had a stake in the company than I thought because, a month after we got bought, most of the management has left to do things like sail around the world or buy a winery in France. At the first branch meeting after the sale, we can all fit into the board room. Also, I'm sure it's a handy money-saving thing to not have us congregate at a hotel. We're now being enticed with cheese and crackers from No Frills and a box of fine Canadian wine, instead of charcuterie and shrimp rings. Reg, who is now the branch manager, sits at the head of the table, wearing his favourite Hermès tie, fiddling with his Montblanc pen. He must have gotten a very heavy set of golden handcuffs to still be here. Reg is the definition of coin-operated. Usually, he starts meetings with a corny joke. "That's what they taught us at IBM," he'd say. "They sure knew how to do things right at Itty-Bitty Machine company." This makes me doubly glad IBM rejected me at the MBA recruitment interview.

Today, though, Reg's dad jokes are conspicuously absent. He starts speaking sombrely. "I know it has only been a month," he says, "but there's something going on with the acquisition." Great. Maybe we're being shut down. Reg continues, "It appears that Nynex professional services has been bought by a company called Stillwell. The thing is, Stillwell didn't expect to also get a Canadian firm. But the good news is they see us as an ideal opportunity to expand into Canada. Their president will be here next week. I'll need all project managers to prepare a status deck and a sales funnel forecast."

I look at Tim, who's sitting across from me. He raises his eyebrows. Nobody says anything though. Best not to let Reg know what we're thinking. Cards, chest. What you get when you buy a professional services company is the revenue from work in progress (which will end when the projects end, and may or may not be suitably profitable), a list of customers (which might as well be the phone book), a bunch of revenue-generating units, a.k.a. employees (who can and will walk out the door), and some intellectual property (which may or may not be as brilliant as it purports to be).

When I stop by the office the following Monday to collect my mail, Reg hijacks me in the mailroom. "I think you should have an office," he says. "How about Kathy's old one? It's got two windows." I'm almost done winding down the EDM project. It is being mothballed rather than abruptly cancelled, to preserve the existing artifacts for a future retube reboot. This boils down to a career-nonlimiting move disguised as a noble thought for the Hydro guys. The antique document management software and Windows 3 file formats, if they could even have been found, would have been as useful as driving a Model T in the 401 express lanes.) I don't know what Reg's motive is for offering me an office except it must have something to do with money. My work has pretty much been his meal ticket, and the photo board is looking a little sparse these days.

* * *

A delegation from Stillwell had descended on the Toronto office, and Reg is entertaining them in the boardroom. The grapevine says they've already ordered a new sign for the office door and new stationery with their logo, a stylized, blood-red *S* that looks like a viper chasing its tail. "You have to be kidding," Tim said when I met him for lunch a few days earlier. "They're going to rebrand you guys immediately?" He has already gone to a new firm, the same one a lot of people have joined. "Stillborn will be more like it." He has a point. Nobody in the Canadian market has a clue what Stillwell does. "I also heard they are really more of a body shop than a turnkey project place." I had heard that too, but I told him I'm going to hang in for a while. Turns out document management is taking off like gangbusters. Reg wants me to start up a practice. It would look good on my resume. Maybe. Or maybe not if I'm working for a company with no apparent track record.

    I'm in my office, wondering whether my tenure here is worth bringing in the ballet poster from home, the one showing legs in grubby legwarmers en pointe in even grubbier ballet shoes, when Janet, the new receptionist and office manager, buzzes my phone. "Reg wants you to join the meeting," she says. I ask her if I'm needed for any particular reason. "Probably to fall on a sword, if necessary. Either that or to pour the coffee," Janet says. When I enter the room, a guy from Stillwell is finishing a presentation about the company's mission, values, and core competencies. I guess it's Reg's turn now. I grab a chair at the back, thankful I wore my red power suit today.

Reg starts running his deck with an org chart that shows our Québec City, Ottawa, and Toronto branches dangling off the Montreal head office, followed by a chart showing the revenue breakdown across the branches, and a list of our top ten customers. The Stillwell guys look confused. "Kweebeck?" says a guy in a rumpled suit with a bad comb-over. "Like French people? I thought this was a Canadian company. Isn't this your headquarters? And where the hell is Ottawa?" Uh-oh. Wait until they find out most of the consultants in Québec City don't speak English. Due diligence appears not to be their strength. But then again, I'm guessing we are but a rounding error in the Nynex bottom line.

Reg seems slightly uncomfortable, but nothing would ever part him from his instinct for self-preservation. "Shall I proceed with the revenue numbers, then?" I'm pretty sure this will not go well. About half of the revenue comes from "Kweebeck" projects. We do pretty good here in Toronto, but Ottawa is dependent on federal government contracts, and I'm guessing the proposal award competitions would not look kindly on an American parent company trying to scoop up tax-payer dollars. I think Ottawa will be toast, followed by incineration of the rest of our stale loaf of bread. Reg continues with his recitation of the firm's accomplishments, which is kind of a moot point since Stillwell has already bought us.

The Stillwell contingent silently picks at their Druxy's smoked meat sandwiches, Reg's favourite lunch, presumably processing their predicament. Janet knocks on the door. She has a slip of paper in her hands. "Shelley from your office called to tell me your flight has been moved up," she says.

"You need to leave now if you are going to make it. There is a car waiting downstairs." The Stillwell guys bundle up their briefcases, nod at Reg, and scuttle off to repatriate themselves to a place that would never tolerate two official languages.

Reg puts his pitch slides back in their binder, then looks at me. "Drinks are in order, I think," he says. "Let's see if Janet wants to come." Apparently, Reg and reality have never met.

* * *

For my return to the office "beach project," Reg has asked me to start sifting through dozens of file boxes resulting from cleaning out the offices of the voluntary and involuntary departed. My mission is to unearth intellectual property that can be reused and deliverables we might be able to leverage. Our methodology is officially defunct, since Stillwell doesn't want to license it and pay royalties to the principals that retained copyright, so we have to work from scratch to invent some new IP that will differentiate us in the market. This is important because Stillwell has to accelerate to warp-speed from a standing start if there is going to be any chance of survival. So far, they've shown just enough good intentions to pave the road that goes due south.

Delving into the boxes is kind of fun, though. Since I was never in the office for longer than five minutes, I never paid attention to the projects we'd been involved with. I spend days happily sorting through file folders and manage to salvage some stuff that might be useful. Decision matrices. Template date models for several industries. Proposals. Process model swim lanes. Feasibility studies. No electronic originals, mind you, but at least some solid reusable work products. I'm doing all this in a space where we used to conduct training on the methodology. I never knew this space existed because we hadn't done training for eons. I am sequestered with total freedom to read anything in any file. I'm guessing Reg didn't consider what might be squirrelled away in people's desks, because I've finally reached a box labelled as being from Penny's office. Penny was the closest thing we had to a Human Resources department.

At Imperial Oil, we had a performance review process called the seriatim. Everybody got ranked against everybody else. It was impossible to have two or more people rated equally. The list of employees descended from top to bottom, which determined eligibility for promotion, raises, and number of steps toward the door. However, your rank in the seriatim was as secret as the recipe for KFC's herbs and spices. As it turns out, unbeknownst to me, CTA did the same thing. I have, in my hands, Penny's seriatim file from last year. For a moment, I consider pushing it through the shredder. Then I reconsider. I take out a thin sheaf of papers containing a numbered list in reverse order and flip to the last page. A list of the top fifteen. I scan the names. Brian, Ted, Todd, Ed, Marcel, Doug, Franz, Walter, Harry, then me. At least I made it into the top ten, but there seems to be a bit of a trend to the names that precede mine. None of them have received the Outstanding Contributor award. None of them have always been 100% billable. None of them have ever published a damn thing. None of them are women. All of them play golf with Reg.

* * *

Tim tells me the new company where he works, Brown & Associates, just landed a document management project but have nobody qualified to lead it. "They also want to start a practice. You could pretty much name your price. Come on in, the water's fine!" he says.

Reg has been spending all his time in his office with the door closed, no doubt working his network to land on his feet. I've continued to hide out in the training room, mining for buried treasure no one will miss. Today is my last day, except I have not told anyone. They'd probably walk me anyhow. I wait until I hear Reg lock his door at five o'clock, then I hang out in my hidey-hole for another fifteen minutes to make sure he is really gone. I slide my resignation letter under his door, check my mail slot one last time, retrieve a pile of phone-message slips, and grab my coat.

Halfway down the hall, I stop, turn around, and go back to the mailroom. My photo is at the top of the board, right under a smiling Reg who's holding the winner's trophy from the annual golf tournament. I pull out the pushpin, crumple my Polaroid image, and drop it in the wastebin. Too bad I don't have a lighter. I retrace my steps, lock the front door, and push my key through the mail slot. Bridges officially burned.

I exit the streetcar at Dundas and Sherbourne, stepping over the Pepsi-can crack pipes on the sidewalk. My rescued orange alley cat is on the doorstep, scratching his fleas and complaining about why he's waited so long to get into the comfort of the house. I scoop up the pile of mail from the floor of the front hall and dump it, along with the contents of my briefcase, on the glass coffee table. This is what I have to show for three years of work. All I've salvaged are a few folders of stuff I can use for templates to build my document management practice. There's also the noncompete contract Stillwell sent me. Unsigned. Hard to prove I'm competing when there's nothing to compete against.

I flip through my Day-Timer and six pink phone-message slips flutter down to the Persian carpet. Two are from Tim at Brown & Associates. Four are from The Cat. I walk to the fridge, take out a bottle of wine, and pour myself a glass of yesterday's sauvignon blanc. Then I pick up the phone.

Author's Note

In the 1980s, Toronto was itching to untether itself from its straight-laced persona, just as I was beginning my "real life" as a career girl, which I hoped would be as glamourous as Mary Richards' in *The Mary Tyler Moore Show*. Toronto's path to something more fulsome than booze sequestered behind the counter at the liquor store and restaurants featuring meat and two veg was equally as circuitous as my own. But all was not lost. The early part of the decade heralded the rise of new wave music and the bar scene on Queen Street West. In the middle, dining took a daring turn toward goat cheese on top of salads and sauces made from fruit. The later years were infested with yuppies on an indulgent quest for the best car, the most expensive vacation, the widest ties, and the biggest shoulder pads. Good thing selfies had not yet been invented.

I did not carry a tape recorder around with me, so all dialogue is a recreation of how I remember situations and conversations. I have changed names with abandon, sometimes because the actual names were irrelevant to the story and sometimes just because. In other cases, I kept the character's real name because the real name was important to the story. Like Mr. Bill, for example. And The Cat.

I can attest that everything in this book actually happened, although sometimes, as public service, I have compressed or expanded timeframes because the story just flowed better that way. I have also created somewhat of a pastiche of two consulting firms (both of which are long gone) I worked for during the period portrayed in the book, although I can attest that all of the situations depicted did take place.

I wrote this book for a couple of reasons, the first being I did not want to be that person with only one book in her. The second is that I think there is a lesson to be learned about the dearth of women in STEM careers. Trying to entice binders full of women to take science, technology, engineering, or math degrees is not the answer. The definitive solution to the lack of female women in technology careers is to strip off the credentialism blinders and just hire more women. More artsy women. We can string coherent sentences together. We can think critically. We can ask the right questions. We can kick tech ass.

Acknowledgements

My continuing gratitude to my Tuesday Night Prayer Group, a safe haven for repentant writers, and also a shoutout to Greg, Meghan, Cheryl, and the other fine folks at Iguana Books who midwifed both this and my previous book.

www.ingramcontent.com/pod-product-compliance
Lightning Source LLC
Chambersburg PA
CBHW030108170426
43198CB00009B/535